SATHER CLASSICAL LECTURES
VOLUME SEVENTEEN
1942

THE RELIGION OF GREECE
IN PREHISTORIC TIMES

GLAUKOS AND POLYIDOS
Sotades bowl, now in the British Museum

The Religion of Greece in Prehistoric Times

BY

AXEL W. PERSSON

UNIVERSITY OF CALIFORNIA PRESS
BERKELEY AND LOS ANGELES
1942

UNIVERSITY OF CALIFORNIA PRESS
BERKELEY, CALIFORNIA

CAMBRIDGE UNIVERSITY PRESS
LONDON, ENGLAND

COPYRIGHT, 1942, BY
THE REGENTS OF THE UNIVERSITY OF CALIFORNIA

ACKNOWLEDGMENTS

It gives me great pleasure to express at this time my profound gratitude for the honor shown me in my appointment as Sather Professor of Classical Literature in the University of California, 1940–41, and also to express my joy that it was possible for me to fulfill the obligations of the appointment in spite of difficulties occasioned by the exigencies of wartime.

The lectures are printed substantially in the form in which they were delivered; only references and some small additions are inserted in the text.

Now that they are ready for publication, I wish to express my grateful acknowledgments to all who have assisted me in completing the work and giving it its English expression, especially Mrs. Siv Belfrage, Mr. John Hamilton, Mr. Albin T. Anderson, and Mr. Herbert Diamante. I also feel deeply my indebtedness to my colleagues in the Department of Classics at this University. To Mr. Harold A. Small, Editor of the University of California Press, I owe a special debt for the last careful revision of the manuscript. Finally, to Professor George Karo, now at Oberlin College, I am indebted for a last reading of the proofs.

A.W.P.

Berkeley, California

CONTENTS

	PAGE
INTRODUCTION	1

CHAPTER

I. MINOAN-MYCENAEAN RELIGION AND ITS SURVIVAL IN CLASSICAL MYTH 5

II. MINOAN-MYCENAEAN SIGNET RINGS AND THE VEGETATION CYCLE 25
    WINTER 32
    SPRING 46
    SUMMER AND HARVESTTIME 67

III. DEATH AND RESURRECTION—OFFERINGS AND FESTIVALS 88

IV. MINOAN-MYCENAEAN RELIGION COMPARED WITH THE RELIGIONS OF ASIA MINOR, SYRIA, BABYLONIA, AND EGYPT 105

V. MINOAN-MYCENAEAN SURVIVALS IN THE GREEK RELIGION OF CLASSICAL TIMES 125

VI. THE VEGETATION CYCLE AND THE NORDIC RELIGION OF THE BRONZE AGE—SUMMARY . . . 153

INDEX 183

ILLUSTRATIONS

Glaukos and Polyidos . . . . *Frontispiece*

FIGURES IN TEXT

	PAGE
Urn burials at Sphoungaras	13
Mummies from Mycenae and Egypt	16
A lekythos, now in Jena, showing Hermes Psychopompos standing beside a large storage vessel	18
Decoration on a gold cup from Dendra-Midea	27
Votive steles from Memphis, showing ears and eye . . .	34
Design on a gold ring from Dendra-Midea	40
Mirror from Dendra-Midea, showing, on the wooden handle, the "Goddess with the Mirror"	44
Oriental cylinder seals showing the "Goddess with the Mirror"	45
Oriental cylinder seals showing a seated deity holding in its hand an object, above which is a sun disk	46
Bell-shaped and cylindrical idols from Gazi, Crete . . .	48
Miniature fresco from Knossos, showing the "Sacred Grove and Dance"	50
Oriental cylinder seal showing animals in the attitude of adoration	52
Oriental cylinder seal showing a tree and an animal . . .	54
Oriental cylinder seal on which the feet of the male worshiper are shown apparently as with shoes.	58
Bead seal from Old Salamis on Cyprus, showing a rayed obeliskoid stone	63
Rings from Asine, showing scenes from bull games . . .	66

ILLUSTRATIONS—*Continued*

	PAGE
Painted plaster tablet from Mycenae, showing a figure-eight shield	73
Boeotian plate showing Demeter with poppies and spikes	75
Scene from the "Campstool Fresco" in Knossos	77
Cylinder seal from Babylonia, showing cult boat with man and woman as occupants	86
Fresco from Knossos, showing the somersault performed at a bull game	94
Seal stone showing an athlete swinging himself over the bull from one side to the other	96
Seal stones showing the climactic scene of the bull games	97
Glass plaque from Dendra-Midea, showing "Europa" on the bull, and an Egyptian design on papyrus showing the moon god on the cow	133
Oriental cylinder seals showing the naked goddess above the bull	134
The Ephesian Artemis as shown in a statue in Naples and in a terra-cotta statuette in the British Museum	145
Seal stones from Vapheio, showing a man in Anatolian dress	146
Boat representation from a rock engraving in the province of Bohus, Sweden, with a man and a woman beside the ship	153
Boat representations from rock engravings in the province of Bohus, Sweden, with a man and a woman embracing each other on the ship	154

PLATES

The rings, and scenes depicted thereon, discussed in the text, pages 32–86, in the same numerical order 171

INTRODUCTION

BEFORE we enter upon our announced study, I should like to say a few words about the background against which this problem, like so many others concerning prehistoric cultures in Greece, must be viewed.

To suppose that the great cultures in the eastern Mediterranean area and in the Near East were separated from each other, in the beginning, by the broadest of gulfs is an interpretation wholly at variance with the facts. On the contrary, it has been clearly enough established that we have to deal, in this region, with an original or basic if not completely uniform culture, so widely diffused that we may call it the *Afrasian*.[1] It extended westward as far as Thessaly and southern Italy, perhaps as far as China in the east, and certainly covered a large part of the African continent. While man himself remained in a nomadic condition, this culture could never reach a high stage of progress; yet, for my own part, I would include among its achievements the arts of spinning and weaving, and the art of making and painting pottery, with colors fixed by a second firing. These are common traits which occur throughout all the oldest cultures within the Afrasian region—in Egypt, in Crete, in the Tigris-Euphrates and Indus valleys. Each feature represents an invention or a complex of inventions which we can hardly believe originated independently in different places. Taken together, these single arts coalesce to form a basic unity of culture which was spread throughout this enormous geographical area by wandering hunters and shepherds who, from necessity, led a migratory existence in their perpetual search for prey or pasturage. These wanderers covered far greater distances upon these expeditions than we formerly gave them credit for. It is my opinion, also, that a kind of primitive writing and the use of the seal

---
[1] Cf., e.g., Marshall, *Mohenjo-Daro and the Indus Civilization*, I, pp. 93 f.

were elements of this basic culture, as well as certain religious concepts which I shall deal with presently.

With the gradual introduction of agriculture the great rivers tempted these people to a more permanent form of settlement; and with the sowing and reaping of crops it naturally became important to them to keep other men away from their preserves. Thus out of the old homogeneous culture there arose through this process of conscious severance the great cultures centered around the river systems of Afrasia—and to some degree, I believe, the races developed in the same manner. We find the individualization of great culture groups in the valleys of the Nile, of the Tigris-Euphrates, and on the plains of the Indus. The importance of these river systems was much greater at this time when the plow was still unknown, when wheeled vehicles had not made their appearance and beasts of burden were few, and when the knowledge of fertilizers for the field was still in its infancy; only the periodic floods made hoe agriculture possible and watered the growing crop. The river, at this time, also served as the chief means of communication: it was the artery of trade and the channel of all intercourse.

These various cultures, which were thus originally differentiated from a lower, basic culture, in time formed new connections and again came into contact with each other after their primary separation. Our archaeological finds give evidence of such trade relationships. This should not surprise us, since we should always be prepared to find evidence of such intercultural influence in any culture pattern. And surely the interchange of spiritual goods is no more remarkable than that which involves material commodities.[2] Thus it happens that from the very period with which we are most concerned, namely, the second millennium B.C., hundreds of Egyptian objects have come to light in Greece

[2] For such relations cf. for example Contenau, "Les Hittites, l'Orient, la Grèce," *Revue d'Assyriologie et d'Archéologie Orientale*, XVI, pp. 97 ff.

and similar quantities of pre-Greek wares in Egypt. The finds made at Ras Shamrah in Syria during recent years admonish us to take account of cultural relations of a most intimate nature between the eastern and western lands in prehistoric times.

Against this general background our treatment of the pre-Greek religion must be viewed.

CHAPTER ONE

MINOAN-MYCENAEAN RELIGION AND ITS SURVIVAL IN CLASSICAL MYTH

IT WAS HARDLY more than forty years ago that Sir Arthur Evans began his epoch-making excavations in Knossos on the island of Crete and thereby opened to us an entirely new prehistoric cultural world. The culture which he revealed he himself called the Minoan, after the mythical king Minos. It soon became evident, however, that the prehistoric high culture of the second millennium B.C., which Heinrich Schliemann had discovered in Mycenae some thirty years earlier, was intimately related to this Minoan culture; and thus we have come to speak of a Minoan-Mycenaean civilization as a whole. Subsequent excavations have shown, especially with respect to the earlier history of the development of this civilization, that there is a striking difference between Crete and the Greek mainland. The archaeologists whose field is prehistoric Greece view as one of their most important tasks the differentiation between the two cultures. This differentiation it is sometimes possible to make, especially upon the remains of material culture; as yet, however, it is hardly feasible with respect to the less palpable evidence of the intellectual aspects of that culture. To be sure, I believe that it is possible to detect certain differences, as for example in the forms of the religion; nevertheless, even here I have been reluctant to draw any hard and fast lines of distinction, and have been content to use the old term, Minoan-Mycenaean. I wish, however, to place the weight of emphasis on the term Minoan; the addition of the other word, Mycenaean, becomes necessary when we have to deal also with objects that come from the Greek mainland, though they belong to a time when the mainland was strongly influenced by Crete.

Anyone who wishes to study the Minoan-Mycenaean religion cannot neglect the basic work done by Evans on this subject in his "Tree and Pillar Cult" (*Journal of Hellenic Studies*, 1901, pp. 99 ff.) and the frequent and extensive researches upon its special problems to be found scattered in his *Palace of Minos*. A comprehensive survey of all the material has been made by Martin Nilsson in his *Minoan-Mycenaean Religion*, published in Lund in 1927. This study throws much light upon the archaeological material contained in the reports of all the excavations up to that day; Nilsson illuminates the entire subject with his critical insight into detail and admirable observation of the facts, and he has unhesitatingly discarded whatever seems, in the severity of his judgment, subordinate or foreign. In my opinion he has sometimes been too severe in his pruning of the tree.

More recently the material has been enriched by new excavations. Even we Swedish archaeologists have had an opportunity to bring our bundle of straw to the stack. Indeed, we have been constantly urged forward by the Crown Prince of Sweden, Gustaf Adolf, whose vital interest in archaeological research has continued active even to the present day. Because of his support—even to the point of his personal participation in the field work—it has been possible for us to conduct our excavations in Asine and Dendra-Midea, whence new material has been unearthed, some of which helps to shed light upon our immediate subject.

Moreover, in the earlier treatment of the various representations of prehistoric religion we lacked a systematic approach and an interpretation of the most important pieces of evidence bearing upon our knowledge of this religion, the gold signet rings.[1] These graphic documents, pictures without words, require a thorough interpretation;

---

[1] Their importance was first clearly emphasized by H. von Fritze in his essay, "Die Mykenischen Goldringe und ihre Bedeutung für das Sacralwesen," *Strena Helbigiana*, 1900, pp. 73 ff.

and until now they have never received their due. A precise description of them is necessary, one so precise that the meaning becomes self-evident; as the great master of this art, Carl Robert, says: "Aus einer guten Beschreibung muss sich die Deutung von selbst ergeben" (cf. *Archäologische Hermeneutik*, p. 15). We shall be guided by this archaeological principle in the examination of our material here. But let us first give some indication of the main characteristics of this Minoan-Mycenaean religion as it has been made known to us from the earlier researches.

In this religion the cult of tree and stone, as Evans first pointed out, is a characteristic feature which it has in common with many other primitive religions. Survivals of these early objects of worship, these "stocks and stones," are to be found in classical times by the side of divinities in full human form. We have, as one example, Apollo with his laurel and the omphalos—the sacred stone in Delphi, the "world's navel."

How are we to regard this connection between tree and stone? According to Evans, "the bætylic stone was always at hand as a material home for the spiritual being, brought down into it by due ritual" (*The Earlier Religion of Greece*, p. 13). But this form of possession was itself transitory. The inert object, though sacred in itself, was only "charged"—if we may use Evans' striking expression—with the divinity through invocatory action. Only thus did it become a real "Beth-el," a "house of the Lord." "The sacred tree," says Evans further, "might itself be regarded as permanently fitted with divine life as manifested by its fruit and foliage." Here I would introduce a reservation about this word "permanently." As we shall see, we are dealing with a deciduous tree, which sheds its leaves during the winter, a time at which divinity is not present in it. In a similar manner in classical times Apollo did not deliver oracles at Delphi throughout the year; in summer he retired to Delos.

In the pertinent representations that we shall examine here more thoroughly, we shall see that the tree and the stone are found very often side by side, in the same way that they appear together in the rustic cult of classical times which we find pictured repeatedly in the background of many of the Pompeian wall paintings. I postpone to a later page my own opinion of their significance (cf. below, p. 166).

A religion which did not offer artistically corporeal figures of the divinity must have left greater latitude to the imagination of its votaries when they desired to visualize its anthropomorphic aspects. Both hymns and myths lent material to this end. We may refer, for example, to the Homeric hymns, which were developed during a period when men were still satisfied with comparatively uncouth pictures created by nature herself since the stone had not yet become the image of a god. So far as we may judge at present, the Minoan religion lacked genuinely aesthetic representations of its divinities. But this did not prevent the apparition of the god's presence, or his intervention in man's life through an epiphany in human form; the god is made after man's desire, not man after god's. Often the presence of the divinity may be manifested by a bird. As we shall see, revelation of the divinity through a human form introduces certain difficulties of interpretation since it becomes necessary to determine, each time, whether we are faced with a deity or a human being.

In his discussion of representations of this general kind, Evans has referred to a "Great Goddess" and a "Boy God"; and about these Dr. Hogarth, in his article, "Aegean Religion" (*Hastings' Encyclopaedia of Religion and Ethics*, I, p. 143), has formulated the following internal relationship: "They personified the Supreme Principle as a woman to whom was subordinate a young male, less in honour and probably later in time. There is no evidence for more deities than these. The religion was what may be called a Dual

Monotheism." Nilsson, with his thoroughgoing and sharply critical attitude, does not categorically repudiate this thesis, but rather contents himself with interpreting the monuments from exterior criteria while he leaves open the possibility of the presence of a larger number of divinities (cf. *Minoan-Mycenaean Religion*, pp. 334 ff.); H. J. Rose concurs with Nilsson on this point (cf. *Handbook of Greek Mythology*, p. 46). Recently Marinatos has given good reasons for the unity of the different schemes of revelation of the "Great Goddess" (cf. *Ephemeris Archaiologike*, 1937, p. 290).

We have already hinted that one must postulate certain ideas about the divinities which were given form by myths in prehistoric times. Both Evans and Nilsson have referred to several myths that can still be traced in classical times. I wish to touch on another, which until now has escaped attention but which has provided the point of departure for my own studies. This is the Glaukos myth. Following is the account of this myth given us by Apollodoros (*Bibliotheke* III, 3 f.).

While Glaukos, the son of Minos and Pasiphae, was still a small child, he died from falling into a jar, a pithos, filled with honey, while he was pursuing a rat—or a fly; the manuscripts are uncertain: μῦν or μυῖαν. Upon his disappearance his father Minos made many attempts to find him, and finally went to diviners for advice on how he should go about his search. The Kouretes answered that Minos had among his herds a cow of three different colors and that the man who could offer the best simile for this phenomenon would also be the one to know how to restore the boy to life. The diviners gathered together for this task, and finally Polyidos, son of Koiranos, compared the cow's colors to the fruit of the bramble. Compelled thereupon to search for the boy, he eventually found him by means of his powers of divination. But Minos next insisted that Polyidos must restore the boy to life. He was therefore shut up in a tomb with the dead body. While in this great perplexity, he saw a snake approach the corpse. Fearing for his own life should any harm befall the boy's body, Polyidos threw a stone at the serpent and killed it. Then a second snake crept forth, and when it saw its mate lying dead it disappeared, only to return with an herb which it placed on the dead snake, immediately restoring it to life. After Polyidos had seen this with great surprise, he took the same herb and applied it to the body of Glaukos, thereby raising him from the dead. Now although Minos had his son restored to life again, he would not allow Polyidos to depart home to Argos until he had taught Glaukos the art of divination. Under this compulsion Polyidos instructed the youth in the art. But when Polyidos was about to sail away, he bade Glaukos spit into his mouth. This Glaukos did, and thereby unwittingly lost the power of divination. "This much must suffice for my account of the descendants of Europa," says Apollodoros.

Another version exists in Hyginus' *Fabulae* (no. 136). When Glaucus, the son of Minos and Pasiphae, was playing ball, he fell into a jar filled with honey. Having sought him in vain, the parents questioned Apollo. Apollo answered Minos: "A monster—a beast and a sign—has been born to thee, and he who can find the interpretation of this can also restore your boy." When Minos heard the Oracle's answer, he questioned his people concerning a sign. They answered him that out of his herds a calf had been born which three times a day, every four hours, changed its color; first it was white, then red, and finally black. Minos assembled all the wisemen together, and when they could not interpret the sign, Polyidus, the son of Coeranus, showed them that the monster was comparable to the fruit of the mulberry tree, which is first white, then red, and finally, when ripe, black. Then Minos said to him: "In accordance with the answer of Apollo you are to restore my son to me." As Polyidus continued to study the sign concerning this matter, he saw a night owl perched on a wine cellar, driving away bees from its entrance. Understanding the sign, he drew the boy, lifeless, from the honey vat. Minos then said to him: "Since you have now found the body, you must also return its soul." When Polyidus confessed his inability to perform this task, Minos had him shut up in a tomb—*monumentum*—together with the boy, and ordered that a sword should be placed therein. When they were thus enclosed, a snake suddenly approached the boy's body, and Polyidus, who feared that it might devour the boy, took up the sword and killed it. Another snake then appeared, seeking its mate, and, finding it dead, brought an herb wherewith it touched its lifeless fellow and restored it to life. Polyidus then treated the boy in the same manner, with similar results. Their cries were heard by a passer-by, and Minos ordered the tomb opened again. He received his son unhurt and sent Polyidus home to his native land with rich gifts.

This myth is preserved in this detailed form in these two late sources only, Apollodoros and Hyginus. Remnants of it may also be found in later writers, for example in Lykophron, 811; Tzetzes, Scholia on Lykophron, 798; and in Eustathios, Scholia on Homer, 369, 20 and 894, 42.[2] That the myth, however, is of some antiquity and that the late authors had good sources is best shown by the fact that the subject is dealt with by the three great dramatists. Aeschylus treated the material in *Kressai*, Sophocles in *Manteis*, and Euripides in *Polyidos*. Aristophanes in turn argued against the philosophical speculations of Euripides on the matter in a similarly named comedy. The story has also given rise to the expression: Γλαῦκος πιὼν μέλι ἀνέστη (Apostolius, Cent. V, 48), "Glaukos rose from the dead after he had drunk honey." The myth was also produced in the

[2] Cf. Kirchner s.v. "Glaukos," in Pauly-Wissowa, *Real-Encyclopädie*, VII, p. 1415.

form of a pantomime, according to Lucian, *De saltatione* 49. According to a version briefly referred to in the Scholia to Euripides, *Alkestis* 1, and in Hyginus, *Fabulae* 49, Glaukos was restored to life by Asklepios instead of Polyidos.

A proof of the story's popularity in the days of the great dramatists is contained in the famous representation on the Sotades bowl, now in the British Museum (see frontispiece, above, after Pfuhl, *Griechische Malerei u. Zeichnung*, no. 526). It is a polychrome drawing done on a white background with extraordinary elegance and delicacy. Considered as a picture, the representation is, as Pfuhl has pointed out (cf. *ibid.*, II, p. 547), decidedly naïve. The artist has given us a huge *tymbos*, a grave mound, in section. We can see clearly that Glaukos and Polyidos are placed not before, but within the mound, but unless we were familiar with the story we should not understand that the diviner with his staff, or lance, actually aims it at one of the snakes. There is also a certain naïveté in the representation of the boy, who does not appear to be as one dead; rather, the crouched position in which he is pictured gives the impression of a cowering living being who watches the preparations being made for his own revival.

Let us now attempt to analyze this myth. The significance of the names of the two principal figures is clearly evident: Glaukos is "the gray-blue one," Polyidos is "he who knows many things."

The first act or incident deals with Glaukos, the son of Minos, who dies when he falls into a large storage vessel containing honey. Preller has already stated (*Griechische Mythologie*, 3d ed., II, p. 475), with reference to this, that it is "ein Ausdruck für einen frühen Tod, bei dem das Bild vom Honigfass der im Orient nicht ungewöhnlichen Sitte die Verstorbenen in Honig beizusetzen entlehnt ist." I agree with Preller in believing that the expression "to fall into a jar of honey" is to be identified with "to die"; but I am of the opinion that the expression has a more precise meaning, namely, that it is a direct reference to the practice of burying the dead in honey.

The custom of burying the dead in large storage vessels or pithoi is of widespread occurrence during the Middle Bronze Age throughout the Aegean culture area. It is to be met with both on the Greek mainland, in the Cyclades,

Fig. 1. Urn burials at Sphoungaras.

and in Crete (see fig. 1, after Edith Hall, *Excavations in Eastern Crete, Sphoungaras*, Univ. Pennsylvania Museum Anthropological Publ., III, 2, pl. XI).[3]

In Asia Minor, however, this form of burial was even more common and at times was the only form practiced, as for example in Yortan and at Alishar-Hüyük, in levels I and II, which are provisionally dated as of the period between 3500 and 1750 B.C. It is probable that this peculiar form of burial spread from this area to the Greek world and on to central Europe, where it occurs, although somewhat less frequently, in the Aunjetitz culture. Even in other respects Anatolian influences must be assumed in explaining

[3] For the pithos burials, cf. my explanations in *Asine, Results of the Swedish Excavations 1922–1930* (Stockholm, 1938), pp. 349 ff.

peculiarities in this culture (cf. G. Childe, *The Danube in Prehistory*, pp. 239 ff.). I am not, of course, unaware of the fact that similar urn burials have occurred in some parts of the Americas, and that some Indian tribes in South America even now practice this method of interment (cf. Eric von Rosen, *Popular Account of Archaeological Research during the Swedish Chaco-Cordillera Expedition, 1901–1902*, p. 2 and fig. 4; C. B. Moore, "Aboriginal Urn-Burial in the United States," *American Anthropologist*, VI, pp. 660 ff.). In America, too, the custom probably spread from one center.

Now, since the custom of pithos burial after the end of the Middle Bronze Age is to be met with only sporadically in the Greek culture area, occasionally in eastern Crete, in the Dipylon necropolis, and at the periphery of the world of Greek culture, there seems to me some reason for suspecting that this detail of the Glaukos story is of Minoan or pre-Mycenaean origin.

In my discussion of the grave materials of the Middle Helladic period in the records of our excavations in Asine, I have sought to show (cf. *Asine*, pp. 350 f.) that during this period there prevailed a custom of burying, in pithoi, small children, imperfectly embalmed in honey, and thus have attempted to trace the use of honey in the cult of the dead from this source. The significance of honey in the cult of the dead in classical times is well known (cf. Stengel, *Opferbräuche der Griechen*, pp. 183 ff.). A connecting link is to be found in Homer between the later honey offerings to the dead and the funerary practice which I have assumed for the Middle Helladic period. At Patroklos' funeral, vessels containing honey were among the objects placed upon the pyre (*Il.* XXIII, 170), and we find the same procedure in the story of Achilles' funeral (*Od.* XXIV, 68). Of this custom of placing vessels filled with honey around the dead on the pyre, Helbig says that it is "höchst merkwürdig" (*Das Homerische Epos*, p. 56). He soberly points out that they could hardly have served any practical purpose, since honey, not being inflammable, as oil and fat are, would not aid in the burning of the body. And he then questions whether its use is not to be explained by assuming that honey played an important role in burial methods during pre-Homeric times. For my part, I am convinced that this was the fact.

We must assume that a simple embalming process was essential in the intramural burials during the Middle Helladic period, when the dead were either laid in earthen graves just below the floor—or, if dead children, in pithoi, when they were buried in a room,—or buried within the house in a cist, the upper part of which might lie only a few inches below the surface and which sometimes was actually level with the floor. For such kinds of embalming, honey proved an excellent and convenient natural preservative: the wax made the body airtight, and the sugar drew the moisture from the corpse and thus dried it. Preller has rightly emphasized that this usage was widely diffused throughout the Orient; Herodotus (I, 198) says that the Babylonians were accustomed to bury the dead in honey. And the use of pithoi for burial purposes certainly reached Greece from the Orient. Even Lucretius was apparently conversant with the practice in his own day. He says (III, 889) that it is of no consequence whether, after death, a man is torn asunder by wild animals, suffers cremation, *aut in melle situm suffocari*. Pliny (VII, 35 and XXII, 108) refers to the preservative properties of honey. It is also generally known that Alexander the Great was embalmed in honey after the custom of his Asiatic predecessors, a process which was especially necessary when his dead body was to be brought from Babylon to Alexandria for burial (cf. Statius, *Silvae* III, 2, 118; Curtius, *Alexander* X, 10).

The only conclusive proof that has yet been found for embalming in the prehistoric period in Greece was discov-

16 THE PREHISTORIC RELIGION OF GREECE

ered in Shaft Grave V in Mycenae. Since this find has had small recognition, and as Schliemann's description seems to me extremely important, I shall take the liberty of quoting verbatim from his book, *Mycenae* (pp. 296 ff.).

"Of the third body, which lay at the north end of the tomb, the round face, with all its flesh, had been wonder-

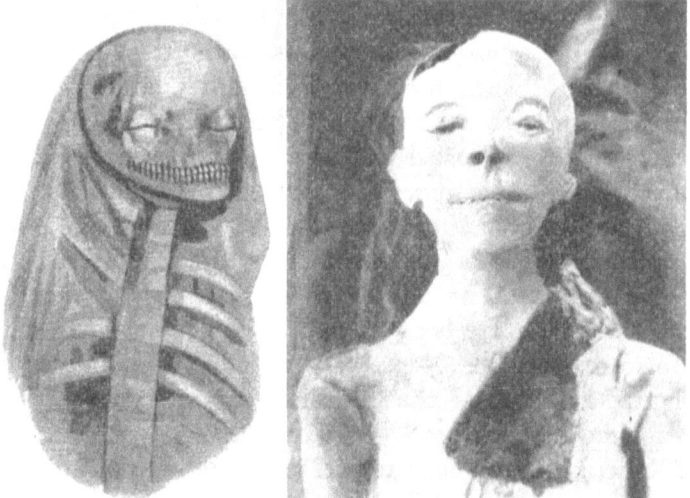

Fig. 2. Mummies from Mycenae and Egypt.

fully preserved under its ponderous golden mask; there was no vestige of hair, but both eyes were perfectly visible, also the mouth, which, owing to the enormous weight that had pressed upon it, was wide open, and showed thirty-two beautiful teeth. . . . The nose was entirely gone. . . . The color of the body resembled very much that of an Egyptian mummy. . . . But, nobody being able to give advice on how to preserve the body, I sent for a painter to get at least an oil painting made, for I was afraid that the body would crumble to pieces. Thus I am enabled to give a faithful likeness of the body as it looked after all the golden ornaments had been removed." His figure 454 reveals a mummified head (see fig. 2); a comparison may be made with an Egyptian mummy head from Elliot Smith's "Egyptian Mummies" (*Journal of Egyptian Archaeology*, I, p. 193, pl. 32, fig. 1) (see fig. 2). That the mummification at Mycenae was not more perfect is not surprising when we remember that the art did not reach its full flower in Egypt until the beginning of the New Kingdom (cf. Elliot Smith, *ibid.*, p. 193).

Helbig (cf. *Das Homerische Epos*, pp. 55 f.) also wishes to infer evidence of the preparation of the corpse from the fact that the word ταρχύειν is employed in three places in the *Iliad* with the significance of "to bury," the later form ταριχεύειν meaning "to preserve, to dry, to embalm." From one place in Herodotus (IX, 120) we also see that the ancients regarded the bodies of the great heroes as τάριχοι, mummies. And the fact that Hector's body was placed on a *lit de parade* for nine days (*Il.* XXIV, 664), that of Achilles for seventeen (*Od.* XXIV, 63), also speaks in favor of a process of preservation; as likewise the treatment Thetis administers to the body of Patroklos in order to preserve it: she shed ambrosia and red nectar through his nostrils that his flesh might abide the same continually (*Il.* XIX, 38 f.). As Helbig has rightly emphasized, this does not give the impression of a poetic fiction, but refers most certainly to an actual process in the preservation of the body.

It is of interest to note that one of the meanings of the word pithos during the classical period was "the kingdom of the dead," Hades. The frequent, often humorous, stories which are connected with the pithos or storage vessel in later mythology show how widespread this idea must at one time have been (cf. Gruppe, *Griechische Mythologie*, p. 816). It is pertinent in this connection to remind ourselves of the appellation of the first day of the *Anthesteria* festival in Athens, which was known as the *Pithoigia*, that is, the Opening of the Pithos. The Anthesteria forms the connecting link between the Cult of Dionysos and the Cult of the Dead. It is believed that the Pithoigia was limited to the worship of Dionysos, and that the observances on the third day, the *Chytrai*, referred only to the dead. The usual theory about the Pithoigia holds that this day is so named

Fig. 3. A lekythos, now in Jena, showing Hermes Psychopompos standing beside a large storage vessel.

because the new wine was then broached and drunk for the first time (cf. Deubner, *Attische Feste*, p. 94). I am myself of the opinion that behind the Pithoigia there lies originally something of a different nature, namely, the "grave opening," the recall of souls from the realm of the dead; the festival closed, as is known, with the cry: "Out, ye souls! It is no longer Anthesteria!" I will not, however, deny that the festival in its classical form received a kind of significance from its connection with the Dionysos cult.

We are also reminded, among others, of Eurystheus, who hid himself in a large vessel when Herakles approached with the Erymanthian boar—translated into common speech, he became "deadly afraid,"—and of Ares, who was held prisoner in a vat. The Danish scholar Blinkenberg in an interesting study, "Hades Munding" (*Danske Videnskabernes Selskab*, 1919, II, 5), has dealt with some part of our evidential material and especially with one representation on an Attic lekythos, now in Jena, in which Hermes Psychopompos may be seen standing beside the mouth of a large storage vessel the greater part of which is buried in the earth (fig. 3). With a short staff he directs four souls, winged eidola; of these, two are already high above the mouth of the pithos, one is just flying up, and the last is evidently being forced back by Hermes and is to be seen flying head downward into the jar.

The references quoted above may suffice to show that in the Glaukos myth we are entirely justified in agreeing with Preller that the expressions "to fall into a pithos" and "to die" are synonymous.

The next feature of the myth to claim our special attention is the interesting description of the cow—or calf, according to Hyginus—which had the power of changing its color daily. The solution of the riddle presented by the changing colors can hardly be of any significance in the general account of the myth. But bear in mind the animal here, to which we shall have occasion to return later.

Another detail, however, which requires our attention is the mulberry tree, or, as it appears in Apollodoros, the bramble, which is obviously interwoven into the myth.

The owl which sat near the wine cellar and chased away the bees from the jar which contained honey, and in which Glaukos had died, must also be remembered. It reminds us of the epiphany of the Deity in the form of a bird in prehistoric times. Aelianus (*Nat. anim.* V, 2) relates that a sea eagle which came flying from over the waters and settled on the coast first showed Polyidos that the boy was not drowned, but had died on land.

In the incident relating that Polyidos was shut up with the dead child's body in a *monumentum*, or, according to Tzetzes (Scholia), in an οἴκημα, to reanimate the corpse, we may be certain that we have to deal with some form of grave construction. One is tempted in this connection to consider with Kirchner in his article on Glaukos (in Pauly-Wissowa, *Real-Encyclopädie*, VII, p. 1415) a beehive tomb or similar burial chamber of the type to be met with in Crete during the Minoan period, for example the Isopata Tomb.

A full parallel to the snake and the life-giving plant is to be found in Pliny (*Hist. nat.* XXV, 14) and in Nonnos (XXV, 451 f.). Both relate that in Lydia there was once to be found a snake the mother of which had restored it to life with the aid of a plant, and that later the same plant was used to revivify the divine youth and national hero, Tylos, who had been killed by a snake. Tylos is represented on a coin from Sardes driving Triptolemos' snake chariot and strewing corn on the earth beneath him. This wonderful plant, Διὸς ἄνθος, is called *balis* or *ballis* by Pliny (cf. also *Etymologicum Magnum*, p. 186, 34). Further details are contained in Jahn, *Berichte der Sächsischen Gesellschaft der Wissenschaften*, 1851, p. 133. The life-giving snake plant is also to be met with in pure folk saga; examples are to be found in Grimm, *Kinder- und Hausmärchen*, No. 16, and Frazer, *Apollodorus* (in the Loeb Classical Library), App. VII, pp. 363 ff. It is also undeniable that the original meaning of these saga-invested myths merely referred to the sudden death of vegetation and its revival. It seems to me very probable that the snake is to be regarded here as the symbol for both the destructive and the life-bringing forces of water; we have the familiar swamp dragons, the hydras, *la Tarasque*, and the like. The parallel Tylos–Triptolemos is worth bearing in mind.

According to Apollodoros, Polyidos was compelled to teach his magic art to the revived Glaukos, but upon his departure he ordered Glaukos to spit in his mouth and thus deprived him of his newly acquired divine power. A parallel to this episode is to be found in Servius' Scholia to the *Aeneid* (II, 247), where Cassandra's magic art is turned to evil ends when Apollo spits into her mouth. This is also a well-known motif in folk sagas (cf. Grimm, *Deutsche Märchen*, 1056, and Jahn, *Berichte der Sächsischen Gesellschaft*, 1855, p. 85). The significance of this episode in the Glaukos myth is clear: the demonic power which Glaukos had received departs from him and returns to Polyidos when he spits into the latter's mouth.[4]

According to Preller, the Glaukos myth is based upon an ancient diviner's saga, and its allegorical content portrays the triumph of the diviner's art in all its three functions: the solving of riddles, the foretelling of the future from the passage of birds, and the knowledge of cures. In his view, which is typical of his time, Glaukos is regarded as "vermutlich ein Bild des Morgensterns" (*Griechische Mythologie*, 3d ed., II, p. 475).

However, we have scarcely the right to view this legend apart from the others in which a Glaukos figure also occurs. Like many other Greek myths and legends, the original Glaukos myth has been mixed in later times with motives taken from pure folk saga. Sometimes the mixture with other material is so strong—and this applies especially to the Glaukos myth in Boeotia—that one has been tempted to distinguish various Glaukos figures. To me, this seems hardly justified. The connection is revealed in certain details.

Glaukos from Anthedon, "the city of the flower (or

---

[4] For the literature concerning the importance and significance of saliva in magic, cf. Gruppe, *Griechische Mythologie*, p. 887; C. de Mensignac, *Recherches ethnographiques sur la salive et le crachat*, Bordeaux, 1892.

herb)," a small town on the northern coast of Boeotia, is a typical Minoan-Mycenaean creation, a composite being—human and fish, or human and snake,—and he there becomes a special sea god; at Potniai, in the interior, he is especially associated with horses. In Anthedon the Glaukos legend is connected aetiologically with the name of the city, and it is related that an herb once grew there which, if eaten, gave immortality. Glaukos is set forth as the son of Poseidon or Kopeus, an eponym for the Kopais lake. It is said in the legend that Glaukos was a fisherman from Anthedon who once saw the fishes which were thrown up on the beach restored to life through the touch of a plant. He tasted the plant and, as one version tells, became mad; as another relates, was changed into a sea god and leaped into the sea; or, as a third says, became immortal but grew old and therefore leaped into the sea—he is sometimes identified with Ἅλιος γέρων, "the old man of the sea."

The wonderful plant is undoubtedly the same that grows only on the Isles of the Blessed and is that with which Helios nourished his horses; it was the divine grass sown by Kronos and given to Anthedon by the special favor of the gods. Here the plant which appears in the original legend plays a leading part, and the figure is developed consequently. Glaukos, "the gray-blue one," is identified with the smooth and gray-blue sea before a storm—he becomes a diviner; wisdom and age follow—he becomes "the old man of the sea."

The cult of Glaukos is known from Anthedon, from Potniai, in Delos, in Gytheion, in Corinth, and among the Iberians. We can trace a cult connection with Ariadne on Naxos from Euanthes (in Athenaios, VII, 296 c), and according to Theolytos (*ibid.*, 296 a) he was taken prisoner in her dwelling by Dionysos and bound with vines.

Glaukos in Potniai is, according to the Corinthian saga, the son of Sisyphos, king of Corinth, the founder of the

Isthmian games and father of Bellerophon. He kept his mares between Plataiai and Thebes, but was torn asunder by them in Potniai or at Pelias' funeral games when he was thrown by them from his chariot. The cause of the horses' fury is variously explained: they either ate a special plant or drank from a sacred spring, or they were prevented from mating by Glaukos and thus caused Aphrodite to become enraged, or they were unable to procure their usual fodder of human flesh. This saga has surely come to Corinth from Boeotia, where it had its beginnings, the plant in Anthedon and the horses in Potniai.

Later, Glaukos was transferred to Asia Minor, where through his son Bellerophon he becomes the progenitor of the Lycian noble families and lives again in his grandson and great-grandson of the same name. The latter, with Sarpedon, was the leader of the Lycian allies of the Trojans.

Our own Glaukos was the son of Minos and therefore had his origin in Crete, while Glaukos from Anthedon was, according to one version, the son of Kopeus and was for this reason connected with the center of the Minoan power on the mainland, in Boeotia. It thus becomes clear why he is later connected with the Cretan Ariadne, and we also come to understand why a Glaukos occurs at the side of Minos' brother Sarpedon in Lycia, since according to Herodotus (I, 173) the Lycians were invaders from Crete. The snake and the life-giving plant occur in Lydia as well.

With these components of the Glaukos myth in mind, we may now venture the statement that the dead boy who was bitterly mourned and later restored to life, the tree, the life-giving plant, the serpent, and so on, appear to us unmistakably as different elements derived from an ancient vegetational religion. For the very fact that Glaukos was the son of Minos, that a cow or a calf takes a part in the story, and that Glaukos himself was closely related to Ariadne, should indicate to us that the legend must be treated together with the pieces of evidence which we have at our disposal concerning the Minoan religion. These are, to be sure, as was indicated earlier in our inquiry, representations; but several of these representations appear to me to be in the form of pictographs, pictures, that is, to be read and translated—provided, of course, we have a certain knowledge of the material. An interpretation of this material, supplied us by our Minoan-Mycenaean gold signet rings, is, I hold, absolutely essential for any knowledge of the religious ideas of that very period. This being so, we will now turn to the "textbook" of the Minoan-Mycenaean religion.

CHAPTER TWO

MINOAN-MYCENAEAN SIGNET RINGS AND THE VEGETATION CYCLE

EVER SINCE the discovery of the first gold rings in Mycenae, it has been apparent that one group of them, indeed the largest one, bears representations of a religious nature. The Glaukos myth prompted me to examine one of these representations more closely; and this limited investigation has since led me to undertake a more detailed study of the group as a whole.

But before we proceed further, a word of introduction on the nature and composition of these representations may be pertinent. Evans, in *The Palace of Minos* (I, pp. 685 ff., III, pp. 156 ff.), has demonstrated that the engraved representations on the gold rings are partial copies of, or translations from, related scenes upon the Minoan-Mycenaean friezes or frescoes. By tracing back a scene such as that on the Ring of Nestor, he has shown how it would actually have appeared as a frieze. The one attendant difficulty here, namely, that the authenticity of Nestor's Ring may be doubted upon good grounds, does not invalidate the strength of his argument or the justice of his conclusions. His views on such or similar representations are now generally accepted (cf., e.g., Martin Nilsson, *Minoan-Mycenaean Religion*, p. 551). If additional proof is demanded, one has merely to consider the great gold ring from Tiryns (our ring no. 24; see plates beginning on p. 171), on which the figures represented are joined together on a purely architectonic frieze as the carrying element. To extract, and portray in miniature form, a larger pictorial representation was obviously attended by difficulties, as may be seen, for example, on the ring from Vapheio (our ring no. 3), where on the extreme left a pithos has simply been cut away in the representation on the signet bezel. Limitation of space is often the reason for the violent postures which some of the figures adopt. The posture on a rectangular field would not need to appear thus contracted. The strongly bowed yet well-incorporated trees which follow the elliptical surface must be ascribed to the same cause.

On a number of signets we have also to reckon with the reproduction of several frieze zones at once. Consider the large Tiryns ring (no. 24). We have not only the architectural frieze below and the main frieze with figures, but also, higher up, a frieze with the sun and moon. The undulating line of division between these two last frieze scenes or extracts is also to be met with on the painted friezes, for example on the miniature frescoes. With this composition before us, we can understand the representation on the large gold ring found in a hoard at Mycenae, with the sun and moon above an undulating line which is interpreted as the sky (in no. 22). If we imagine the entire representation in the form of a fragment of a frieze, we have on the elliptical surface a band of constant height below the sky. Only where this surface is broadest was there room for a small part of an upper frieze with the sun and moon, which was thereupon incorporated. Thus we may obtain a natural explanation of this peculiar composition as a whole.

Now, with regard to the concept of space, the Minoan-Mycenaean artist was familiar with two sorts of perspective: in the representation of figures, whether of man or beast, he sometimes used what we may call a style with true perspective; the other may be called the bird's-eye or cavalier perspective. In vase painting these correspond respectively to what Furumark has called "zonal decoration" and "unity decoration" (cf. *Studies in Aegean Decorative Art*, p. 13), and Matz, "Streifenverzierung" and "Flächenmusterung" (cf. *Die frühkretischen Siegel*, p. 169). This so-called bird's-eye or cavalier perspective may be best explained thus: the ground is reproduced as seen from above, and therefore stretches from the lower to the upper edge of the representation; but all objects on that ground are given as seen from the side, as a flying bird, or, better, a horseman on his mount, sees the ground and the objects

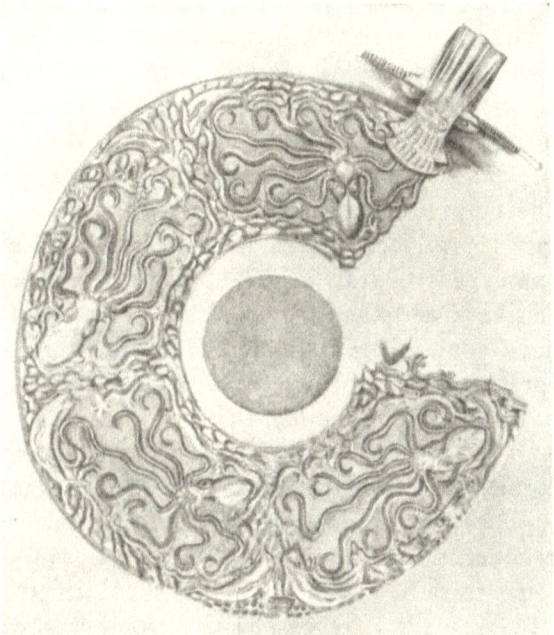

Fig. 4. Decoration on a gold cup from Dendra-Midea.

on it. In fact, it is this same striving to reproduce the different elements of a representation from the most characteristic angles, at the sacrifice of realism in the whole image, that is found in all primitive art. Let me refer to the gold cup (fig. 4) which we found in the Royal Tomb in the course of our excavations at Dendra in 1926 (cf. *The Royal Tombs at Dendra Near Midea*, pp. 43 ff.). Four octopuses with twining tentacles are depicted within a framework of coral with sea anemones and the stones and sand of the sea bottom. Six dolphins are apparently diving from the upper margin, where ten argonauts are depicted. What is characteristic of the presentation here is that the bottom of the sea is seen from above and therefore stretches from the lower to the upper edge of the representation, precisely as on the gold cups from Vapheio. The sea bottom is the background against which the artist wished to represent living things and on which he added all manner of related detail, coral, sea anemones, octopuses, dolphins, shells. He drew each object from its most characteristic aspect. Many objects are most effectively represented from a side view—and so here. The octopuses presented a special problem. Their bodies are reproduced therefore as if seen from above—they are most easily drawn thus—but the arms are viewed from the side so as to show their disklike suckers. The dolphins and argonauts are all depicted in profile.

In representations of the kind we are dealing with here we have to take into account, therefore, a picture surface parallel to the spectator and not a ground sloping backward. Against this parallel surface all perpendicular objects are given in profile.[1] This point of view by which representation is governed must be kept in mind.

In interpretation, to be sure, we are not justified in viewing in divers ways a representation composed of many figures, but must content ourselves, and quite rightly, with regarding it as a plane upon which all things, human figures, trees, plants, and symbols, are displayed. The figures are commonly distributed upon their field to avoid overlapping. Depth, the third dimension of a true perspective, was not sought after.

In judging the representations on the gold rings, if we consider their design to be derived from that of the friezes, the question will arise whether the different frieze scenes

---

[1] V. Müller has admirably dealt with the question of the forms of spatial conception in his paper, "Kretisch-Mykenische Studien. I. Die Kretische Raumdarstellung," *Archäologisches Jahrbuch*, 1925, pp. 85 ff.

were strictly divided from each other or whether we have to reckon with a continuous or flowing representation. The second view appears to correspond with the facts. On the long friezes from the palaces in Tiryns and Mycenae this continuity of representation is clearly shown. In the strict time sequence of events, the successive scenes extend in a linked succession round the room in the form of an interrelated mural decoration without any dividing lines; thus we see the departure for the hunt, on foot and by chariot, the hunt itself, and finally the climax, the capture of the prey; or again, the preparations for war, the harnessing of the horses to chariots, the armed departure, and the battle itself, as well as the siege of a stronghold (cf. Rodenwaldt, *Tiryns*, II, pp. 234 f., and *Fries des Megarons von Mykenai*, pp. 59 f.). We have in these friezes, even if the same persons cannot be said with certainty to be represented in the different tableaux, a means of representation which is very similar to that customarily described as "simultaneous representation of successive events." In any case, we have displayed for us a large, continuous, pictorial narrative. In the representation on the small gold ring from Tiryns (ring no. 25) we may assume a similar form of representational art, and perhaps also on another of the gold rings (ring no. 7). L. Curtius rightly speaks (*Festschrift Paul Arndt*, p. 42) of an original "aufzählende, additive Reihe" which occurs in both primitive and child art, and of which we have numerous examples from the Orient and from Egypt. Later this tends to disappear, and is replaced by a contracted and more truly proportioned organization of design, more in keeping with the growing sense for order and condensed expression.

For this reason, representations such as occur on our rings are usually but the core of events removed from the frame of larger motives and made independent. The representation is, so to speak, condensed, and then established as a closed composition; this makes it possible to force it into a limited space, elliptical, as on our gold rings, or quadrangular, as in the metopes.

How, then, shall these representations on the gold rings be viewed? Should the engraving on the ring, or the impression to be taken from it, be considered as the criterion by which to judge the primary purpose of the representation? That is, did these rings serve purely as ornaments to be worn, or were the seals used to denote ownership? That we are concerned here with true signet rings intended for practical use is pretty certain. We have several impressions in clay which can almost definitely be traced back to gold rings (Evans, *Palace of Minos*, IV, p. 607). Indeed we possess a whole series of impressions on clay lumps, sealings of documents, from one and the same ring, all found together in the North Columnar Wing of the little shrine on the west side of the Central Court in Knossos; the impressions show the goddess standing on the mountain peak between her guardian lions (*Palace of Minos*, IV, p. 596, fig. 597 A, e). Evans has advanced the theory that what we meet with here proves that the ring was worn and used by some religious functionary. A ring of this kind has been considered as of individual ownership—a sign of the wearer's dignity, which was buried with him, "a kind of passport to the world beyond," as Evans expresses it. The rings which bear cult representations are often badly worn, a proof of their long and diligent use. In my opinion, therefore, we must regard the impression to be taken from the ring as the desired end result of the artistic engraving, that is, a positive embossed representation, not a negative, *en creux*.

I do not believe that we are justified in drawing far-reaching conclusions from such details as, for example, whether a worshiper raises the left or the right hand in greeting. Let me point out that on our ring no. 13 the worshipers in the engraving on the ring are turned to the left with the right hand raised, while the actual impression which the signet yields, as you can observe, shows them facing to the right with their left arms raised. Tsountas (in *Revue Archéologique*, 1900, p. 13) has pointed out that such a stamped image would be bizarre, and has been tempted to conclude that this ring served not as a seal, but as an ornament; however, I am inclined to believe that this detail might be due quite simply to convenience of composition.

With respect to the representations of figures, we often meet with the ancient type in which the composition is on a bilateral frontal plane, similar to the symbolical arrangement of a heraldic coat-of-arms. In arrangements which include large figures, these are most frequently placed in the middle. When there is a series of figures on the seals and signet rings, the arrangement in the impressions usually runs from left to right. This is true also of most of the cut stones with animal representations, as Schweitzer has rightly pointed out (cf. *Deutsche Literaturzeitung*, 1931, p. 72). This also argues for the fact that the impression is that which was desired from the ring, since in this way we have a parallel to the youngest system of the Cretan script, Linear B, in which the signs always face the right and in which the reading of the script from left to right is beyond all doubt. But one must not emphasize this agreement too strongly. Examples counter to this also occur in Minoan glyptics, for example our ring no. 20, and the gold ring from Athens, the so-called "Minotaur Ring" (cf. Shear, in *American Journal of Archaeology*, 1933, p. 540, fig. 1). If we consider the friezes which, as already mentioned, formed the background for the representations on the seal rings, their contradictory testimony makes it appear that we lack any general rule. One may only say that in general practice it seems most probable that an orientation from left to right was preferred on the gold rings, and one from right to left on the frescoes.

Having made these general remarks concerning the spatial conceptions and the nature and execution of the representations, let me now proceed to an interpretation of our gold rings, which I wish to present in a particular order of succession.

Vegetation Cycle: Winter

Ring no. 1.—In the Ashmolean Museum, Oxford, there is a gold ring which, according to the information obtained by Professor Nilsson (cf. *Minoan-Mycenaean Religion*, p. 296, n. 3), was left to the museum as a gift by Mr. Warren. Dr. Hogarth, sometime Keeper of the Museum, stated that Mr. Warren knew of its existence "almost as long as the contents of the Vapheio Tomb have been known." The close connection between the representation on this ring and another discovered in the Vapheio Tomb (our no. 3) renders it extremely probable that this ring once belonged to the contents of this tomb. The illustration given here is taken from a cast (see plates beginning on p. 171, which picture the rings in numerical order).

We are shown a kneeling woman bending over a large storage vessel of the type which was used in pithos burial. Her left arm, bent at the elbow, rests on the rim of the vessel. Her head, inclined forward, is supported by her left hand, and she thus presents an attitude of mourning. She is making the gesture of speech with her right hand; note the outstretched fingers! To the right of the vessel may be seen a large, elliptically rounded stone, with the leafless branches of a tree or bush behind it. The broad, wavy line behind the woman's back, ending in a triangular figure above the right shoulder, is possibly the loop of a sacral knot; but I prefer to interpret it as plaits of hair, comparing it to the similar representation of hair on the standing female figure farthest to the left. It is not wholly impossible to interpret the wavy line and its triangular terminal as a snake with a clearly defined head; we have such a representation on another ring (no. 8). In the empty space above the mourning woman a large ear and an eye occur. Behind her, to the extreme left, a richly clad female figure is to be seen with wavy hair, vehemently gesticulating; the left hand is raised toward the left shoulder, the right forearm is stretched outward. In the upper part of the empty field between the two women is a smaller male figure rigidly posed, a bow in the horizontally outstretched left hand and a smaller object in the uplifted right. The lower limit of the picture is determined by a podial-like stage: a long, horizontal line with a number of smaller vertical lines, perhaps indicating the surrounding wall of a *temenos*, a sacred place (cf. nos. 15, 16, 18), perhaps only an indication that the representation was taken from a mural fresco.

Both Evans (*Palace of Minos*, II, p. 842) and Nilsson (*Minoan-Mycenaean Religion*, p. 296) consider the small figure, high in the picture, as the young male partner of the great Mother Goddess, whom Evans recognizes in the female figure on the left. It is now generally accepted that this great goddess is the real divinity of the tree cult (cf., e.g., Schweitzer, *Gnomon*, 1937, p. 15, and Malten, *Hermes*, 1939, p. 198). I cannot share Nilsson's view of the ear and eye (cf. *Minoan-Mycenaean Religion*, pp. 276 f.), namely, that they have significance here as mere amulets. Numerous parallels are known of similar representations from Egypt, accompanied by explanatory texts, for example in Petrie, *Memphis*, I, pls. IX ff.; I refer particularly to pl. XI, 15, which shows two ears before Ptah, with a text which says "Ptah hears the prayer"; another, pl. XII, 22, with six large ears placed above hands raised in prayer, bears the same inscription. Another plate (XIV, 33) shows a votary carrying offerings to Ptah, and in the space above a large eye appears (fig. 5). The significance of the ear and eye is perfectly clear in these representations; the god hears man's prayers and sees his gifts.

In referring to the whole representation upon our ring, Evans says that it is "not easy to explain," and Nilsson confines himself to a comment upon the small armed god, who is merely said to be "in the air." But the moment we realize that the vessel depicted actually signifies a pithos

Fig. 5. Votive steles from Memphis, showing ears and eye.

burial, the whole scene becomes entirely clear. We have, then, the familiar theme of sorrow over death, and the well-known symbolism, as for example in the cult of Adonis, where the dead is first wept over before his later ecstatic and joyful resurrection. The pithos is placed close to the tree and the stone—note that the tree is leafless! The ear and the eye signify that the gods have heard man's lamentations and seen his sorrow; their epiphanies are to be seen behind the back of the mourning woman. Thus we have a double representation of the two central divinities in the Minoan religion, the aniconic forms before the sorrowing woman with the pithos, and their epiphanies behind her. The dead shall arise!

Ring no. 2.—A seal ring, poorly preserved, from Phaistos was published by Savignoni in *Monumenti antichi*, XIV, pp. 577 f. An enlarged photograph is reproduced here, taken from his impression (pl. 40, no. 6). All the features of the reproduction are indistinct in detail.

In the center a man is to be seen bent over an object tapering at top and bottom which has been described by all who have examined the picture as a stone, but which should surely be interpreted as a pithos (for a burial pithos of the same form cf. *Asine*, p. 121, fig. 99). The man's head is inclined, so that he appears to look down into the object, both his hands being outstretched toward it. He is naked except for a tight-fitting loin cloth and a girdle and bindings around his shins. At the far right a tree is to be seen within an enclosure. A woman grasps its trunk with both hands, as if to shake it. Both her legs are bent at the knees, the left raised somewhat higher than the other to simulate violent movement. She has been described as wholly naked, but upon closer examination it will be seen, from the thickening of the right thigh, that she is wearing a man's loin cloth. From the tree, here in leaf, a curved line of dots extends horizontally, probably falling leaves or fruit.

On the extreme left an apparently tall, narrow, elliptical baetyl, or "una tavola betilica," is to be seen, which seems to be composed of a smaller horizontal plate placed over a sacred stone. The peculiar shape of the stone may perhaps be interpreted as the outer half, together with the upper horizontal part, of an enclosure around a tall, narrow stone—the left part of the vertical figure. Just to the right of this, and behind the two human figures, a bird is shown in the ordinary flying posture; its body is seen from the side, the wings and tail from below. The ground is indicated by a line at the bottom of the picture.

Here also we may see an instance of mourning over a pithos burial. The woman on the right who is violently shaking the tree is, by doing so, attempting to attract the attention of the divinity who is in intimate association with the tree. I am inclined to give this interpretation to all the scenes in which a tree is more or less violently shaken by human figures. It should be remembered that touching or grasping as a means of transferring power in a purely magical way plays an important role in all primitive religions; it was thus that the sick and diseased touched the robes of Jesus. The embodiment of divine power in a tree is paralleled in the dryads of classical religion; if one cut or hewed down a tree, one wounded or killed the tree's spirit. In like manner, violence of movement was in classical times the means whereby one sought to attract the attention of the gods; thus, to address the gods of the underworld, one stamped upon the ground (cf. Stengel, *Die griechischen Kultusaltertümer*, 3d ed., p. 80).

But to return to our ring. The flying bird may be taken for the customary sign of the epiphany of the god; compare the dove of the Holy Spirit! The bird omens of antiquity are intimately connected with this. (For the epiphany see Nilsson, *Minoan-Mycenaean Religion*, p. 288.)

We have reason to pay particular attention to the peculiar dress in which the two actors appear: the man in tight-fitting loin cloth with bindings around the shins, the woman in the male loin cloth. These very details will be found again on later representations, and we shall be able to draw important conclusions from their occurrence.

Ring no. 3.—An extraordinarily interesting ring belongs to the finds made in the Vapheio Tomb. It was first published by Tsountas in *Ephemeris Archaiologike*, 1889, pp. 170 f., and is here illustrated from his photograph of the cast (his pl. x, no. 39).

We begin our interpretation at the extreme left. Here a leafy tree may be seen growing from rocky ground. Below it is depicted the greater part of an upturned pithos, not a "baetylic pillar," as it has usually been described (cf., e.g., Evans, *The Earlier Religion of Greece*, p. 29). Tsountas himself rightly described the object as a large vessel, but believed that the tree grew up from within it. A reconstruction of the whole vessel (our no. 3, *a*) shows clearly that it must be regarded as inverted, with the mouth downward. Below the vessel to the right a stony terrain is also given. Upon this a man is represented as if climbing over the rocks. His right arm is raised, and apparently he grasps one of the branches of the tree. His left arm, directed downward, is bent at the elbow, with the forearm raised. He is distinctly wearing a loin cloth; and note the girdle around his waist and the bindings on his shins. His hair falls freely in long locks over his back. Behind him a woman appears, moving to the right. She is clad in a long, flounced skirt; but the upper part of her body is naked, as is usual in cult representations. Her left arm is outstretched, the right bent at the elbow. Plaits of hair, represented in the conventional manner by dotted lines, are to be seen on either side of the head and along the upper contours of her arms. She appears to be in violent motion, and is probably dancing. Above her is to be seen a peculiar object which Evans interprets as a butterfly chrysalis, seeing in this a symbol of immortality (cf. *Palace of Minos*, III, pp. 140 ff.). Above this object a leafy branch is displayed. On the extreme right lies a figure-eight shield, to the left of which are two objects which have given rise to many different interpretations. Evans has wished to see in them a mourning woman, Nilsson a "cuirass" represented on a small scale (cf. *Minoan-Mycenaean Religion*, p. 138). We must regard them as undoubtedly a pair of the so-called sacral knots, fringed on the lower borders, of the kind with which we are familiar through the faience knots from Knossos, from Shaft Grave IV in Mycenae, and from, for example, "la petite Parisienne" from Knossos. In the highest section of the empty space (the

38 THE PREHISTORIC RELIGION OF GREECE

upper right), an ankh-shaped variant of the double axe is represented. The ankh-sign is, as we well know, the common Egyptian symbol of immortality, but it is also met with as a similar symbol in the Hittite region (cf. Bittel, *Anatolian Studies Presented to William Hepburn Buckler*, 1939, pp. 9 f.).

The inverted pithos reminds us of the burial jars from Sphoungaras (cf. text fig. 1, p. 13). We must note that the jar is here placed in the shade of the tree, and it is quite probable that ordinary burial jars were so placed whenever they were not buried inside a house. The role which the tree plays in burial places in different religions, for example in both Christian and Mohammedan cemeteries today, may be brought into connection with the life-giving forces once believed to be found in the tree. Pithos burials of small children inside the houses arose from the belief that the soul of the dead child would soon be regenerated in a new child.

For the religious aspect of the Minoan shield see Evans, *Palace of Minos*, III, pp. 314 ff.; for the ritual use of knots, *ibid.*, I, pp. 430 ff. Nilsson, *Minoan-Mycenaean Religion*, pp. 349 ff., has sought, in my opinion unsuccessfully, to divest the shield of any sacral significance, regarding it as purely ornamental; furthermore, I do not join in his skepticism concerning the sacral use of the knot, *ibid.*, pp. 137 ff. We shall return to these two objects later. The female dancing figure in the middle suggests an orgiastic cult rite. The ankh-shaped double axe and the chrysalis, according to Evans' interpretation, contain a promise of resurrection.

Ring no. 4.—We now proceed to a gold signet ring from Mycenae, reproduced here after a cast published by Furtwängler, *Antike Gemmen*, pl. VI, 3.

To the left stands the bowed figure of a mourning woman bent over an enclosure composed of vertical and horizontal posts with garlands between the two foremost vertical supports. Within the enclosure, in the foremost opening, is to be seen a tall, narrow baetyl, with a small figure-eight shield in the rear. The woman is clad in a flounced skirt. Her hair, depicted in the usual manner by a dotted line, flows down her back. A leafy branch appears above her. Farthest to the right stands a tree, also in leaf, inside an enclosure, closed at the base, open at the top, in which likewise a tall and narrow baetyl is to be discerned.

A man clad in a loin cloth, almost in a kneeling position, with averted face, seems to grasp the trunk of the tree. The strongly bent legs and the backward-turned face give him the appearance of violent movement; he is probably dancing. A woman in a flounced skirt is to be seen in the middle, facing right, with hands on hips. The hair is represented horizontally above her upper arms. She also appears to be in the animated motion of some ritual dance. Between and above the two dancing figures two curved lines may be distinguished (shown faintly on our copy), evidently representing the firmament; we have parallels to these in our representation no. 22. At the bottom of the picture a rough surface is shown, perhaps indicating a surrounding wall of a temenos.

The enclosure over which the mourning woman on the left is leaning is generally believed to be a tomb. The tall, narrow, phallos-like stone occurs as a gravestone in Phrygia, on Attis' grave and elsewhere. In this connection Evans refers to Zeus' grave at Knossos and to the omphalos-like stone with bands around it, which he has recognized on a mural painting from the Palace of Knossos; cf. *Palace of Minos*, II, pp. 838 f. The grasping of the tree in order to attract the attention of the great Tree Goddess, and the orgiastic dance, we are already familiar with from the previous representations.

Ring no. 5.—Upon our excavation of the Queen's tomb in Dendra in the summer of 1939, we found a large number of gold objects, including a signet ring with a religious representation, hitherto unpublished and here reproduced from the original (ring no. 5; cf. fig. 6).

On the extreme right, within an enclosure, is to be seen a small tree with budding leaves and an elliptical baetyl. To the left of the enclosure two women appear, clad in flounced skirts and both depicted in about the same attitude. The lower half of their bodies is represented in profile,

Fig. 6. Design on a gold ring from Dendra-Midea.

turned to the left, their torsos *en face*, with the heads again in profile but turned toward each other. The hair is represented in the usual style. The right arms are bent, with the hands raised; the left arms are stretched downward. The streaming hair, the position of the arms, and so on, clearly indicate the movements of a ritualistic dance.

On the extreme left we have a low building of isodomic construction, apparently in two sections with projecting cornices. I interpret this as a tripartite cult building seen in profile, of the type known from the gold plates found in Mycenae and Volo and from the mural paintings in Crete (cf. Bossert, *Alt-Kreta*, 3d ed., nos. 188, 189). Behind the cult buildings is to be seen the upper part of a column, with its capital, and a little to the right of this a complete column resting on a base, similarly surmounted by a capital. A double entablature rests upon the columns, joining each to the other, and on it two horns of consecration are placed directly above the complete column.

In the intermediary space between the high column and the lower cult building indistinct traces appear of a worshiper, facing the altar and with the left arm raised; in the right hand, which is held in front of the lower part of the body, she seems to hold some object. She is evidently wearing a hide dress around the lower limbs, the tip of an animal's tail being visible behind her legs at the side of the column base, and the bodice is decorated with a broad diagonal band. She is to be compared most closely with the officiating women on the Hagia Triada sarcophagus (cf. Bossert, *Alt-Kreta*, 3d ed., nos. 250–252). A ground line under the columns and the foremost of the dancing women unites the representation.

In view of the small proportions of the isodomic structure, clearly indicated by the comparative size of the female figures, I would remind you of parallels from Knossos (cf. Evans, *Palace of Minos*, II, p. 524), namely, a clay seal impression showing part of a shrine and a worshiper who is considerably taller (*ibid.*, fig. 326), and a clay matrix from a signet (*ibid.*, II, p. 767, fig. 498) showing the goddess seated on a small pillar shrine. A shrine of the same kind as that on our ring, with a similarly massive isodomic structure with a projecting cornice, occurs on the so-called "Ring of Minos" from Knossos; cf. Evans, *Palace of Minos*, IV, pp. 947 ff., where the goddess is represented seated on the upper middle part of the shrine with her feet resting on one of the lower wings. There, the shrine is also obviously smaller than the goddess. The model supplied by the Miniature Fresco from Knossos cannot, to judge from the surrounding figures, have been much more than 2½ meters high, somewhat less than the columnar shrine of which Evans has found traces on the west side of the Central Court at Knossos (cf. *Palace of Minos*, II, p. 806).

Under such circumstances there can be no question of a building in which a cult ceremony takes place; the ceremony is being enacted in front of the building. Probably the main object in the building was an aniconic representation of the deity; in the pillar shrine, a pillar. The building has certainly been imitated from the dwelling house common in Crete; cf. the house faiences from the Town Mosaic, Evans, *Palace of Minos*, I, pp. 301 ff., fig. 223, and the gold plates showing Cretan influence. On our ring this building and the colonnade visible behind it are mutually related, as is evident from the fact that the horns of consecration, the sacred symbol, are placed on the latter, not on the shrine itself, as is usually done. In such an instance as this one readily takes the building for an altar, and we actually have altar structures built in the same manner with square blocks and a covering slab projecting a little beyond the stone structure, thus forming a cornice; cf. for instance a fragment of a stone pyxis from Knossos, there crowned by horns of consecration, Evans, *Palace of Minos*, II, p. 614. As to the question of the horns of consecration and the façade of the Minoan shrine, see in addition Nilsson, *Minoan-Mycenaean Religion*, pp. 140 ff.

We have here evidently a sacrificial scene in connection with an ecstatic dance. The tree with the budding foliage and the baetyl inside the enclosure indicate the actual conditions in closer detail. The hide dress is of sacral use; cf. Nilsson, *Minoan-Mycenaean Religion*, pp. 132 ff. Its significance at the funeral sacrifices is demonstrated by the Hagia Triada sarcophagus; but here, as elsewhere, we have to take its presence into account in the cult of fertility with which the death cult has many other rites in common—the officiating priest clothes himself in the skin of the sacrificial animal. The donning of animal skins is a particularly widespread practice both on classical soil and elsewhere. In the Indus culture, just as in the Sumerian and Babylonian, we find gods and priests provided with horns and tails. The Egyptian king is often represented with an ox tail. I interpret the Minotaur of the Cretan Saga—the Bull of Minos, half man, half bull—simply as the priest-king, Minos, clothed in the skin of the sacrificial animal, presiding over the cult and officiating at its rites. The animal skin, as an important element in weather magic, is retained in classical times, for example at Halos in Thessaly and in Magnesia.

Ring no. 6.—A gold ring of unknown origin, now in the Berlin Museum, first published by Furtwängler-Loeschcke, *Mykenische Vasen*, and reproduced here after a galvanoplastic copy, is said by Evans and Nilsson to have come from Mycenae, but I can find no verification of this statement.

To the extreme left is seen a small cult building, apparently resting upon a raised podium. Inside the building a column occurs with tripartite capital, standing on a clearly marked pair of horns of consecration. Upon the building two other horns of consecration appear. Sitting before this, probably on a low stool, is a woman with her back to the building. She wears a long, flounced skirt, and evidently her upper body is naked. Her right arm rests on her knee, and the hand hangs loosely downward. In her raised left hand she holds a round, handled object which can hardly be anything but a mirror. Before her stands a woman in a similar skirt, also with upper body naked, and decorated with a necklace. She raises the right hand in a gesture of adoration; the left arm hangs straight downward. The two women have their hair done up upon the head. Behind the second figure we see a leafless tree.

The woman in front of the shrine is generally believed, and rightly, to be the epiphany of a goddess. Nilsson speaks (cf. *Minoan-Mycenaean Religion*, p. 305) of the "Goddess with the Mirror," who is here greeted by a devotee. Concerning the object in the hand of the goddess there can be no doubt that it is a mirror, since we now have an exact duplicate on a mirror handle of wood (fig. 7), found in Chamber Tomb No. 2 in Dendra; cf. *Royal Tombs*, p. 96, fig. 71. Nilsson has sought a religious significance for the mirror, but can only refer to the fact that it is "one of

Fig. 7. Mirror from Dendra-Midea, showing, on the wooden handle, the "Goddess with the Mirror."

the Japanese regalia and is said to be the symbol of the sun." He adds: "This example is not only solitary but also far-fetched." For my own part, I have found the "Goddess with the Mirror" much nearer in space and time on representations from Syro-Hittite reliefs and seal cylinders. She is, for example, seen at the side of the great weather god Teschub on the relief from Zendjirli (cf., e.g., Contenau, *Manuel d'archéologie orientale*, II, p. 987, fig. 681). On seals (cf., e.g., Delaporte, *Musée du Louvre, Catalogue des cylindres orientaux*, II, pl. 90, nos. 15, 16) she is often represented sitting on a tabouret with a mirror in her hand (fig. 8), attended by her maidens or receiving gifts from worshipers. Here we have the prototype of "la toilette de Vénus" of later Greek vase painting. As to the composition, one may compare it with other representations (cf. fig. 9) in which the sitting figure holds an object—often inter-

Fig. 8. Oriental cylinder seals showing the "Goddess with the Mirror."

preted as a cup—in the outstretched hand, immediately above which is a clearly marked sun disk (cf., e.g., Ward, *Cylinders and Other Ancient Oriental Seals in the Library of J. Pierpont Morgan*, pl. x, nos. 62, 65). I think the connection is clear enough. The mirror may also occur as a solar symbol. We must remember that the mirror in question is a plain, circular, shining disk of metal. I would also refer to a votive relief dedicated to Jupiter Dolichenus, now in the Altes Museum, Berlin. Jupiter sits enthroned on the left with a double axe in his right hand. Before him, to the right, stands a woman with a mirror in her right hand. I can add another parallel, namely, on the rock engravings in Scandinavia, where sun disks with handles often occur, with which man evidently attempted in some magical way to make the sun rise. We shall return to this later.

Fig. 9. Oriental cylinder seals showing a seated diety holding in its hand an object, above which is a sun disk.

Vegetation Cycle: Spring

Ring no. 7.—A gold ring in the Museum in Candia, first published by Nilsson, *Minoan-Mycenaean Religion*, pl. 1, 4, is given here after his cast.

Our representation (see plates beginning on p. 171) shows, at each end of the engraving, an enclosure in which is a tree with scanty foliage. Facing the tree at the right is a woman in a flounced skirt, her upper body naked and her hair hanging down her back. She leans somewhat forward and grasps the trunk of the tree with both hands. Inside this enclosure there is a tall, narrow baetyl. The enclosure around the tree on the left is divided in the middle by a vertical line, and in the rectangular fields on both sides are chevrons, which probably are to be regarded as garlands. Nilsson, *Minoan-Mycenaean Religion*, p. 230, thinks of "closed double doors"; but see ring no. 4, where garlands are certainly present. The figure near this tree is, like the other, a woman in a flounced skirt, with naked upper body and hair down her back; but she appears in profile, with her back to the tree, and extending both arms upward as if in adoration of a similarly clad woman in the middle of the picture but on a more elevated level. The latter turns her head toward the worshiper and lifts, as if in greeting, her right arm, which is bent at the elbow. Below her is a plant, evidently a triple-cupped lily.

We have here an unmistakable picture of the epiphany and the adoration. It has been suggested, too, that this ring gives us the simultaneous representation of two successive events: the woman to the right, who grasps the trunk of the tree, is thereby attracting the attention of the deity; in the scene to the left we see the result of her ritual action: the goddess has appeared before her.

Ring no. 8.—In the small tomb at Isopata, Evans discovered a ring which in some respects bears a similar representation. The illustration given here as 8 *a*, is taken from a copy of the ring reproduced in Bossert, *Alt-Kreta*, 3d ed., fig. 400 *g*; the positive impression, 8 *b*, is taken from Evans' drawing, *Tomb of the Double Axes*, p. 10, fig. 16.

The scene depicted is evidently in the open air—in a flower-strewn meadow, if we may judge from the plants, which are apparently a species of lily resembling the asphodel. They are four in number and are scattered over the open field shown on one half of the representation. The attitude of the central figure, a woman in the familiar Minoan cult dress, is quite comparable with that of the woman in the middle of the preceding representation, though somewhat more lively. Both hold the left arm (in the cast) downward, though inclined away from the side, and the right arm bent at the elbow. The upper part of the body, and especially the head, are more strongly inclined to the left in ring no. 8; this is required by exigencies of

Fig. 10. Bell-shaped and cylindrical idols from Gazi, Crete.

space. Moreover, this figure is mounted on a higher plane, and below her is to be seen the same lily plant but here more fully developed than in ring no. 7. To one side another woman in the middle of the preceding representation, but not extended upward in adoration; the posture may easily represent her as dancing. These two figures are not turned toward each other. On the opposite side, two women are depicted in profile, both extending their arms upward in adoration, probably directed toward the woman in the middle. Above the foremost worshiper is to be seen a very small female figure of peculiar aspect, showing only one leg and a short ballerina skirt, almost bell-shaped. She is to be interpreted as an idol of the bell-shaped type (cf. fig. 10; and Marinatos, *Ephemeris Archaiologike*, 1937, pp. 278 ff.), placed in the background. The undulating line above the worshipers' upstretched hands is to be regarded as a snake the head of which disappears over the border of the representation. On the other side of the central figure a second snake is to be seen gliding over the dancer, and above the snake a leafy bough is depicted. Beneath the snake's tail and between the two women who face to the front, a human eye is reproduced in the same fashion as in ring no. 1.

We obviously have here the special Minoan conception of space—the bird's-eye or cavalier perspective. We are therefore not justified in regarding the area around the snake as ground, that around the small idol as air; and neither ground nor air would suit the pictured eye. Quite simply, the spectator is parallel to the given field, on which the depicted objects are freely disposed.

What is portrayed is the epiphany of the great Nature Goddess in a spring setting. The eye indicates that the goddess is aware of her votaries—that she regards with satisfaction the ritual dance and the adoration paid to her. This dance scene has an excellent parallel in the Miniature Fresco (fig. 11) of the "Sacred Grove and Dance" from Knossos (cf. Evans, *Palace of Minos*, III, p. 67). The leafy bough here, and on several later representations, should be identified as "Der Maizweig," representing the potent force of vegetation. Usener has called it *ein Augenblicksgott*, "the momentary apparition of the divine"; but it returns regularly every year and consequently can be regarded with equal justification as a symbol of the god who manifests himself in the cycle of vegetation; ἐνιαυτὸς δαίμων, according to Miss Harrison, *Themis* (*passim*). If so, then the snake must be directly related to fertility and the reawakening of life in the spring: it is at this period that it creeps forth from its hole. It may be interpreted as the life-giving force of the water, the quickening rains of spring. We shall return to the small idol later.

Fig. 11. Miniature fresco from Knossos, showing the "Sacred Grove and Dance."

Ring no. 9.—A poorly preserved ring is known from Phaistos, published by Savignoni in *Monumenti antichi*, XIV, pp. 585 f.; the photograph given here is from a cast illustrated in pl. 40, no. 7.

On the extreme right is to be seen a column with its capital indicated by two parallel lines, possibly an abbreviated representation of a sacred building in accordance with the well-known artistic practice of *pars pro toto*. In front of the building, and sitting on the ground, which is represented here by several small embossings, is a seemingly naked female figure, which we must, however, if we note the swelling on the left thigh, visualize as clad in a short skirt; compare our later representation, no. 21, of the woman in "sacra conversazione," of whose position she reminds us in certain respects. The present figure holds her arms bent at the elbows and both hands evidently raised. Before her, placed in an upright position, is a dog-headed, long-tailed animal with drooping paws imitating the conventional posture of adoration; its hind legs are missing. the animal is clearly cynocephalic. Behind it, a woman in a long, pleated, and flounced skirt raises her right hand in the same gesture of adoration. In the space just above the animal a peculiar object appears. The first commentator believed it to resemble the form of a lituus, "ma che anche, specialmente se si guarda in senso orizzontale, richiama inevitabilmente quella dei genitali virili." But Savignoni did not take into account the dot which is so near the larger object. It seems quite plain to me that we have here again a large ear of the same kind as in the first representation. To the right, above this object, is a leafy bough. Strewn about in the upper part of the picture are some misshapen dots. As in some of our other representations, these appear to indicate the ground; which is to say, we are here dealing with a bird's-eye perspective.

Thus once more we have the goddess sitting before her temple in the springtime, as is indicated by the leafy bough, receiving the prayers and worship of man and beast, to which she lends ear. The cynocephalic animal reminds us directly of Anubis in Egyptian representations—the ear points to Egypt, as we have previously observed,—but even were it probable that the figure was of Egyptian origin, we possess closer parallels in Asia Minor and in the Orient. I refer in particular to a cylinder seal reproduced in Eduard Meyer's *Reich und Kultur der Chetiter*, p. 63, fig. 52, where together with human figures we see two erect animals in the same attitude of adoration, the forelegs raised before a divine figure further emphasized by an adjacent sun disk and crescent moon (fig. 12). On cylinders of the Morgan collection we again see the same animal (cf. W. H. Ward, *Cylinders and Other Ancient Oriental Seals in the Library of J. Pierpont Morgan*, pls. XXIX-XXX, nos. 213, 221, 229, etc.; also Chapouthier, "À travers trois gemmes prismatiques," in *Mélanges Gustave Glotz*, I, pp. 197 ff.

Ring no. 10.—A gold ring from Mycenae is here reproduced after an illustration in Bossert, *Alt-Kreta*, 3d ed., fig. 399 *k*, from a galvanoplastic copy.

Fig. 12. Oriental cylinder seal showing animals in the attitude of adoration.

At the far left, around a tree, is an enclosure—I believe it to be constructed of four corner supports held together by a horizontal framework—which rises from the lower part of the terrain indicated around the construction. The lower section of the tree trunk appears to be thickened; we are to understand, I judge, that a baetyl stands in front of the trunk, yet within the enclosure. Nilsson has interpreted this erroneously (*Minoan-Mycenaean Religion*, p. 228) as a central column, and therefore would have us see an altar table with a central support. But the column does not extend up to the horizontal framework, below which we can discern the tree trunk. It is closely reminiscent of the baetyl on our representation no. 4, even though the perspective of the enclosure here differs from the other, where we can see only the foremost supports.

This tree is in relatively rich foliage. Facing the tree stands a man clad in trunks, with bindings around his shins.

His left arm is bent, the forearm extended across the chest. The right arm, similarly bent, is outstretched toward the tree, the branches of which he appears to grasp. Behind him is a wild goat, an *agrimi*, with long horns, represented by dots close to the head and by protracted curved lines toward the extremities. Apparently, a similarly leafy tree grows from the agrimi's back. Nilsson believes that the trunk of this tree has been omitted from under the agrimi's belly. But in my opinion we must here again consider the bird's-eye perspective, especially since several swellings behind the agrimi can be interpreted as signifying the ground. The lower border of the picture is marked by a ground line.

The aniconic deities here represented in the tree and the baetyl are being worshiped by the man in shin bindings. The presence of the wild goat requires an explanation. The constellations which characterized the beginning of spring were the Ram and the Bull, both of which may be regarded as personifications of the impulsion to mate which animals feel in the spring. Animalistic personification of this kind was common, particularly in Egypt; but its intended significance here is certainly less narrow, and is derived from the primitive herder's or farmer's observation of the natural behavior of his domesticated animals in spring.

Ring no. 11.—Tsountas published in *Ephemeris Archaiologike*, 1888, p. 180, a small gold ring from one of the chamber tombs in Mycenae, which is reproduced here from his pl. x, 42.

To the left, as well as on the upper border, a rocky terrain is clearly indicated. Toward the left-hand edge, at the very base, appear naked boughs, and above is a small leafy tree. To the right of these stands an animal; Tsountas says an antelope, but it is probably a wild goat, an agrimi. It has turned its head backward by a strong twist of its exaggeratedly long neck.

Without our preceding representation, this scene might not easily reveal its religious significance. Actually it is an abbreviated version of the engraving on ring no. 10, in which the man and the enclosure around the tree are no longer represented. The religious significance emerges more clearly if we compare our representation with a Syro-Hittite seal cylinder (fig. 13) found in Cyprus (cf. Murray, *Excavations in Cyprus*, pl. IV, 53).[2] It belongs to that large group of cylinders which reproduce the sacred tree with

Fig. 13. Oriental cylinder seal showing a tree and an animal.

different animals, such as griffins, lions, goats, or human figures with the heads of animals. Occasionally these cylinders carry one or more signs of script related to the Minoan-Cypriotic alphabet.

Ring no. 12.—In the *Journal of Hellenic Studies*, 1901, p. 182, fig. 56, Evans published a gold ring from Mycenae which was in his own collection. The illustration here is taken from his drawing of the original.

On the extreme left is pictured a structure standing upon a rocky hill. Evans explains the construction as follows: "The shrine itself consists of what are apparently two pairs of slender pillars supporting an entablature consisting of three members—an architrave, a frieze with vertical lines, which seem to represent the continuation of the lines of the

---

[2] A true duplicate (or can it be the same?) is to be found in the Morgan collection; cf. W. H. Ward, *Cylinders and Other Ancient Oriental Seals in the Library of J. Pierpont Morgan*, p. 79, pl. XXIV, no. 168.

columns below, and a wider cornice above" (*ibid.*, p. 183). Nilsson, *Minoan-Mycenaean Religion*, p. 149, agrees with him. For my own part I am inclined to recognize the ordinary tripartite cult building, the *aedicula*, seen (as on our ring no. 5) in side view. The lower "architrave" represents the cornice of one of the lower wings of the building; the "frieze with vertical lines" and the "wider cornice" are related to the side and cornice, respectively, of the elevated central part of the building. Such an interpretation holds equally for similar structures in our representations nos. 13, 14, and 16. On the cornice, at its middle, stand a pair of horns of consecration, and between them is a curved object which must be interpreted as a branch; comparison may be made, for example, with a lentoid of rock crystal from the Ida Cave and other similar representations on seal stones in the *Journal of Hellenic Studies*, 1901, p. 142, fig. 25. Two similar branches rise from the rocky ground, one on either side of the construction. No central column appears. The small dots between the supports are difficult to explain, though Evans has considered the possibility that they are flying birds. To the right of the construction we see a woman clad in the familiar Minoan skirt and with naked upper body and hair hanging in plaits, visible on her right side. The lower part of the body, as the feet show, is turned to the right, the upper appears *en face*, and the head is in profile to the left, facing the structure. She wears a bracelet on the right upper arm. This arm, which is bent at the elbow, is extended toward the construction, with outstretched hand, as if in a gesture of adoration. To the woman's right on a somewhat higher level is a tree in leaf, or possibly a group of trees, the trunk being given in triple form; but compare the one on ring no. 22. The peculiar straight and curved segmented lines which appear at the bottom of the picture possibly represent the ground; note that the tree is growing out of the continuous horizontal line and that even the structure on the left is also raised to the same horizontal height from the rocky surface. The ground to the left is characterized as stony; and we may perhaps interpret the segmented line as representing grass. The curved lines in the field above the continuous horizontal line may similarly represent the ground, since we are still dealing with the bird's-eye perspective.

It is evident that we are concerned here with a worshiper who has decorated with leafy branches the sacred horns of consecration and the cult building. Since the horns are placed on the construction, we may infer that this was a sacred building. Were it not for this representation, we should not understand the processions in no. 13 and no. 14, which are moving toward similar cult buildings.

Ring no. 13.—This gold ring was discovered in a chamber tomb in Mycenae excavated by Tsountas in 1892 and was first published by him, *Mykenai*, p. 166, pl. v, 3. It is here reproduced from his cast, published in *Revue Archéologique*, 1900, pl. VIII, 2.

On the extreme right is to be seen a small building, which Tsountas has already compared to aediculae with gates, as represented on the famous thin gold plates from the Third and Fourth Shaft Graves at Mycenae. The gate on the right is particularly well depicted; therefore the possibility of assuming an offering table with a central support, which would otherwise be suggested, is excluded. In the open aedicula is to be seen a small column with a base and double capital, a more developed form of the baetyl. A pair of horns of consecration stand upon the building, the horn to the left being for the most part obscured by the bent arm of the foremost figure; but the base is clearly evident in our illustration.

Incidentally, we may note that, starting from an unsatisfactory representation of this ring, Dr. Reichel built up his theory of the "Thronkultus."

Approaching the cult building are three figures of like appearance and having the same attitude, with the left arm bent at the elbow and raised, the right arm lowered at the side, and holding objects in their hands. The object in the left hand of the foremost figure has been omitted by the engraver for lack of space. The others evidently bear branches in their hands, except the last, who holds in his lowered right hand an object which Tsountas calls a knife. The typical flounced skirt is worn by all three figures, while the double elliptical lines on the buttocks are reminiscent of the male loin cloth. We must pay particular attention to the representation of the naked upper bodies. This reveals that, in spite of the skirt, the figures are not female; the Minoan artist knew well enough how to represent the female breasts when he so desired. All three figures are explicitly drawn to appear extremely muscular. There can be no doubt that we are dealing with men in women's skirts. The hair is not loose and flowing, but set in close, thick rolls. The lowered arms, bent at the elbow, are adorned with bracelets. The two foremost figures appear to be wearing necklaces, and the two rearmost to be wearing shoes with heels.

Behind these persons is to be seen a peculiar figure, described by Tsountas as "un végétable," but which, so far as I can see, bears a close resemblance to an insect, specifically a bee; attention must, however, be drawn to the small protruding hairs on the "wings" and "body." The lower limit of the picture is indicated by a horizontal line with numerous small vertical lines below.

The representation as a whole is perfectly clear. We have a small cult building with horns of consecration. Approaching this are worshipers with boughs in their hands, who have been identified as women by all scholars but one who have studied the representation; only Max Mayer, in a parenthetical note on the cult building, has indicated a recognition of the fact that they are male: "Mykenische

Beiträge, II," in *Archäologisches Jahrbuch*, 1892, p. 190, n. 5: "Dasselbe Heiligtum erscheint auf einem neuerdings [1892] gefundenen Siegelstein [obviously a mistake, since it is actually a gold ring], wo sich ihm in uniformer Bewegung adorirend drei unbärtige Männer nähern, oberwärts nackt, mit asiatischen Weiberröcken; offenbar Priester." We shall return later to these peculiar figures, who are obviously meant to be eunuchs, as well as to the "bee." Bear in mind that the last of the three men holds in his downstretched

Fig. 14. Oriental cylinder seal on which the feet of the male worshiper are shown apparently as with shoes.

right hand "un couteau ou un objet analogue," according to Tsountas, *Revue Archéologique*, 1900, p. 9. Furthermore, I would point out the resemblance of the feet of the last two figures, for which I know no parallels in Minoan-Mycenaean art, to those of certain figures on Syro-Hittite seal cylinders. Contenau, *La Glyptique syro-hittite*, p. 29, says: "Il est à remarquer que l'art archaïque des cylindres représente volontiers le pied avec les orteils relevés et la voûte plantaire très incurvée, de façon à faire saillir le talon." I give here a representation (fig. 14) from a Hittite cylinder dated by Ward as *ca.* 1500 B.C., showing a goddess in a flounced dress holding a vase from which spout two streams, behind her a female figure with long hair falling over her shoulder, and before her a male worshiper with exactly the same formation of the feet as in our two figures from the Mycenaean signet ring (cf. W. H. Ward, *Cylinders and Other Ancient Oriental Seals in the Library of J. Pierpont Morgan*, p. 97, no. 219; pl. XXIX).

Ring no. 14.—A gold-plated silver ring was discovered by Tsountas in a chamber tomb at Mycenae in the course of his excavations in 1893 and was first published from a cast in the *Revue Archéologique*, 1900, pl. VIII, 3, from which our representation is taken.

Tsountas, like Furtwängler, *Antike Gemmen*, II, p. 25, and Evans, *Journal of Hellenic Studies*, 1901, p. 184, misunderstood the technique employed on this engraved surface. They believed that the bezel was once completely covered with gold and that the lower half of it had since disappeared. Several finds, among others two similar rings from Asine, Chamber Tomb I (cf. *Asine*, p. 371), show, however, that we are dealing with a special technique which was workable in different metals and which made use of color differentiation as an artistic means of expression. The same technique occurs on the inlaid dagger blades and silver cups with gold and niello inlays from Mycenae, Dendra, and other places.

On the extreme right is seen a construction the lower part of which is missing. What we see is two uprights, without capitals, which apparently support an entablature composed of a lower, somewhat shorter plate, and a higher, longer one above this, on which a pair of horns of consecration are placed. The upper part of the entablature reveals a row of small rectangles which can hardly be anything else but the ends of square-cut beams. Evans has called this construction a sacred gateway; Nilsson prefers to see it as a shrine. I refer to my earlier remarks (p. 55).

Toward this structure come three figures whose lower limbs were engraved on silver and have therefore disappeared. They all wear long hair which descends in plaits over the back and breasts and down to the thighs. All are clad in skirts which differ from those represented in the preceding scene in their numerous small vertical pleats. It would appear that all three wear necklaces; the middle figure also wears a bracelet on the elbow of the right arm. The upper part of their bodies is naked. The foremost figure is seen in three-quarter profile as flat-bosomed, but an elliptical raised area marks the former position of the left breast. The left arm disappears behind the figure, the right is bent at the elbow, and the peculiarly shaped hand appears to point to the building or to be carrying some object. The middle figure has the left arm bent at the elbow, inclined upward. The hand is clenched, with the thumb pointing upward. On the naked upper body, which is seen *en face*, appears an unnaturally distended female breast, placed on the left side and seen wholly in profile. The last figure has likewise a naked upper body, seen in three-quarter profile, and an unnaturally developed female breast, placed on the left side, seen sharply in profile. The left arm is concealed by the upper body and the hand of the downstretched right arm also disappears.

Here, too, the representation is clear. In the lowered hands we must imagine, as in the previous scene, branches or some similar objects. I will merely emphasize at this point the gestures of the hands of the two foremost figures, and the Amazon-like representation of the naked upper bodies. We shall return to them later.

Ring no. 15.—A gold signet ring from Knossos is here reproduced from Evans' drawing in *Palace of Minos*, I, p. 160, fig. 115.

On the extreme right is to be seen an enclosure with high wall and gateway; a portal shrine, according to Evans' interpretation. The gateway is composed of jambs of ashlar masonry, continuing to the right in a wall of smaller stones. Above this is a double cornice over which rise the branches of a tree in full leaf. In the opening appears what Evans and

Nilsson considered a free-standing column, with two rings on the shaft, a clearly marked basal plate, and strongly projecting coverplate. My own opinion is that it is a tall standing lamp of a well-known type. To the left of this is a platform extended to the left, of the same kind as the one represented on the first gold ring, and on it stands a high, narrow object which immediately recalls the shaft which supports the double axes on the Hagia Triada sarcophagus and which is there wound round with garlands. It is generally interpreted, and probably correctly, as an obeliskoid baetyl. Immediately to the left of this appears a small male figure, which may be thought of, from the upward-streaming hair, as floating down from heaven. In the outstretched right hand he holds an elongated object, a spear or possibly a bow (cf. the small figure on ring no. 1). To his left stands a woman on the podium which supports the high baetyl. She wears an elaborately flounced skirt and apparently has a small sacral knot "à la petite Parisienne" at her neck; her hair hangs down along her back. She raises both hands before her face, a common gesture of adoration—she is blinded by the god's epiphany. Behind her a rocky terrain is indicated and a bush with almost leafless branches.

The small male figure is evidently connected with the high baetyl and is hailed as representing the regenerated life in nature. As proof of my contention that the object in the doorway is a lamp, I will refer here to a group of objects designated by Evans as "ladle-shaped vessels" and published in his *Palace of Minos*, I, pp. 624 f., which all bear evidence of having been scorched by intense heat. Two of these bear inscriptions and were found in shrines belonging to Middle Minoan III culture levels. That the lamp in Crete as well as in Egypt played a part in cult ritual, I have sought to show in an account of our excavations at Dendra in 1939, which is soon to be published. In fact, it plays the same role, though on a smaller scale, as the great yearly fires lighted at the beginning of spring, and provides an example of sympathetic magic: by creating a source of light and warmth, man could influence the great source of light and warmth, the sun.

Ring no. 16.—This gold ring was discovered in a chamber tomb in the course of Tsountas' excavations at Mycenae in 1895 and is here published from a cast illustrated in Evans, *Palace of Minos*, III, p. 137, fig. 89.

The florid nature of the representation has given rise to various interpretations. Evans interpreted it first in the *Journal of Hellenic Studies*, 1901, p. 183, as a cult scene with a holy tree and a temenos with a via sacra to the shrine in the middle, an interpretation which was accepted by Nilsson, *Minoan-Mycenaean Religion*, p. 151. Evans later, *Palace of Minos*, III, p. 137, and in my view more correctly, came to regard the representation as a cult scene at a sacred spring.

High in the middle is to be seen a construction with segmented base and similarly segmented outer supports, upon which a triple entablature rests. Between the outer supports three plain, rounded uprights appear. I explain this construction as a tripartite cult building, seen in side view (cf. p. 55). On the entablature, which has a conical object in the middle, peculiar objects are to be seen at the ends, possibly horns of consecration, from which on either side hang three curved objects which I am inclined to interpret as branches, as in the scene on ring no. 12, or possibly plants of the same kind as appear on the rocky section farthest to the left. From this construction a distinct dotted line descends, which was first interpreted as a stone setting, but which Evans now holds represents water. I believe that this latter is the more correct interpretation, especially with reference to the pictographic sign to which Evans (*Palace of Minos*, IV, p. 658) has given the name "drop sign" or "rain pictograph" and which recurs on a number of libation vessels of different types. On both sides of the vertical row of drops are two continuous lines which descend in steps outward to the bottom of the representation. Within these, to a height corresponding to the lowest step, two different constructions occur with segmented inner lines and continuous upper border, each containing three dotted rows, possibly indicating the unhewn stones comprising the enclosure around the slender, cypress-like trees which rise above these. Evans calls them doors. On

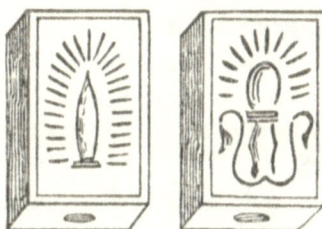

Fig. 15. Bead seal from Old Salamis on Cyprus, showing a rayed obeliskoid stone.

either side of this enclosed area stands a woman, seen wholly in profile and facing the spring and cult building. Both figures are clad in the typical flounced skirt with a pronounced bodice which leaves the breasts naked. Their hair hangs in plaits; their hands are raised in adoration. Behind the woman on the left appears a rocky area with sprouting plants. Behind the woman on the right is seen a tall, slender, elliptical object which is encircled by a ring a short distance from its lower end, and is slightly undulating from there to the top—probably wound with leaves. Around this, like a gloria, is an elliptical row of dots. I am most closely reminded of the shafts wound with garlands on which the double axes on the Hagia Triada sarcophagus are placed, and of a representation (fig. 15) of a rayed obeliskoid stone, the material dwelling place of the solar deity which here is descending upon it, on a tabloid bead seal from Old Salamis on Cyprus (cf. *Journal of Hellenic Studies*, 1901, p. 173). The entire scene on the ring we are here discussing is apparently placed on a stone terrace with two steps, probably an enclosing wall of ashlar masonry (cf. no. 18).

In this instance we have a cult scene which takes place in a free landscape, as the rocky section to the left indicates, with a sacred spring and a cypress grove. The object farthest to the right, quite dissimilar to the two trees referred to as cypresses, in the middle, I interpret as an ornamented baetyl. The representation is unusual in employing the whole landscape as background for this rustic rite, and in certain respects it confirms the interpretation we have given to several details on a signet ring which we have studied earlier (no. 12).

Ring no. 17.—A gold ring in the National Museum in Athens is shown by Nilsson in his *Minoan-Mycenaean Religion*, pl. 1, 2, and is reproduced here from his cast.

Small constructions are to be seen at both right and left, above which protrude scantily leaved trees. To the left appears a man in a loin cloth and possibly with a flat cap, almost kneeling, with one hand grasping the branches of the tree. A woman is seen to the right in a similar position. She is naked except for a clearly marked loin cloth. The breasts are distinctly represented and her hair hangs down her back like a row of beads. Both these figures have their backs turned to a central figure, a woman in a flounced skirt and with her upper body naked, whose head is turned to the left, with arms raised in a lively gesture. Her hair falls down her back.

Nilsson has described the central figure as a dancing worshiper (cf. p. 239), but I believe her to be the Tree Goddess' epiphany, especially when we compare her with the representation on ring no. 1, where the epiphany of the goddess is similarly placed behind the human figures. Indeed, there can be no doubt of it when we take into consideration the position of the small male god behind her. Of special significance in this connection is the dress of the woman to the right. Nilsson has correctly pointed out that the loin cloth which she wears is properly the costume of the female toreadors, but he does not draw the natural conclusion which follows from this. He merely refers to the previously known illustration of the ring shown in our representation no. 2, and believes that this shows beyond doubt a nude woman—but even she, as we have already noted, wears the same form of loin cloth as that depicted on this ring. The natural consequence of this fact and of several other details already described must be accepted and the Cretan bull game admitted as part of the cult's practices.

Ring no. 18.—Evans has published (*Palace of Minos*, III, p. 220, fig. 154) a gold signet ring found in a chamber tomb in the neighborhood of Arkhanes, south of Knossos, which is reproduced here from his photograph of the original.

We see a bull, with high-flung head, in a flying gallop toward the left. An athlete, wearing a loin cloth, is vaulting over the bull. His right hand rests on the bull's left flank, relatively far forward, the left on the bull's right side farther back. In front of the bull is a comparatively large object, which Evans recognizes as a sacral knot, but which I believe, particularly in view of our representation on the Vapheio ring, no. 3, to be a figure-eight shield seen in side view. Below the representation is a "stepped base with isodomic masonry," as Evans says; here undoubtedly a wall enclosing the bull ring. We must also note that the bull is ithyphallic. The representation portrays a well-known scene from the bull games, to which we shall return later.

In Chamber Tomb No. 1 at Asine we found a bronze ring (fig. 16) with a bezel which was half covered with gold plate, the bronze on the other half being left visible. For the technique, compare no. 14. On the gold plate there was depicted the upper part of a bull which evidently was in full gallop toward the left. Parallel with the bull's back is a man wearing a loin cloth and with streaming hair, his right hand resting against the bull's flank, his left on the bull's

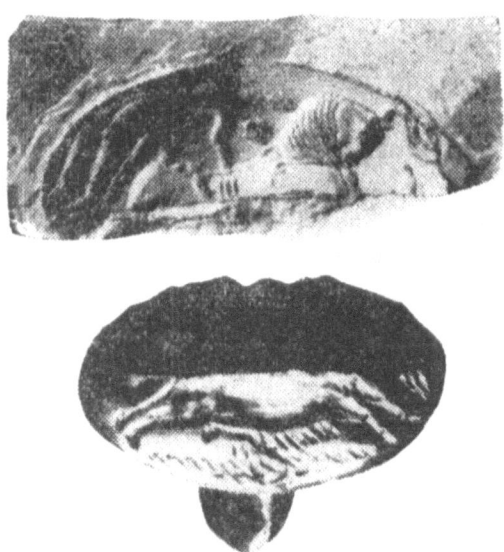

Fig. 16. Rings from Asine, showing scenes from bull games.

neck. The scene represented on our ring no. 18 depicts the action of a moment earlier than that on the ring from Arkhanes, of which it is strongly reminiscent. From the same tomb comes another ring showing the same technique. The upper half of the bezel was of bronze, the lower of electron. On the bronze all details have been obliterated, but the lower part shows that the scene represented was a bullfight. Above the ground, which is indicated by short oblique strokes, a bull—actually no more than the lower part of the animal—is to be seen galloping to the right. The bull's lowered horns, and probably the feet of the athlete, are glimpsed to the extreme right.

Ring no. 19.—This is a gold signet ring from the Smyrna area, published by Evans in his *Palace of Minos*, I, p. 432, fig. 310 *a*, and III, p. 225, fig. 158, and reproduced here after his drawing. The authenticity of the ring may be doubted in respect to some features, but although I have been unable to study the original I will nevertheless include it.

The ithyphallic bull has paused in its gallop to the left and turns its bellowing head backward, watching with interest the athlete who has failed in a difficult leap and is just falling to the ground between the animal's hind legs. The doubtful features are the peculiar coiffure of the athlete and the trunks he is wearing: as a rule, the toreadors are represented with flying locks and wearing a tight-fitting loin cloth. The lower limbs are bound with puttees in the usual fashion. Before the bull two sacral knots—compare our ring no. 3—are depicted, indicating the religious character of the representation. In the upper border a rocky terrain is indicated, since under the bull a beaded line denotes the ground. These geomorphic signs also raise doubts concerning the authenticity of the picture.

Vegetation Cycle: Summer and Harvesttime

Ring no. 20.—A small gold ring, now in Berlin, said to have been found in Kilia in Asia Minor (first published in *Amtliche Berichte aus der Königlichen Kunstsammlung*, 1913, p. 71, fig. 31 *a*), is here reproduced after Martin Nilsson, *Minoan-Mycenaean Religion*, pl. 1, 1; for its origin cf. *ibid.*, p. 228, n. 6.

At the left is shown a sizable structure with a high gateway, the door jambs being represented as single stones. Extending to the left is a high wall, unusually clear in detail, evidently composed of ashlar masonry—compare almost exactly the same thing in ring no. 15. The gateway or entrance is divided down the middle, indicating double doors opening on the enclosure, which in turn is topped along its whole length by a double cornice. A tree sends its leafy branches over the construction.

Before the enclosure stands a man, wearing a loin cloth, who extends his rigid left arm, with fingers outspread, toward a female figure on the extreme right. She wears a wide, peculiarly flounced skirt with bodice and appears to wear a sacred knot, à la "petite Parisienne" below the nape of the neck. The arms are given merely as two stumps, and the head is not clearly visible. Nilsson calls this figure a goddess; but the very appearance of the sacred knot makes this improbable, since, so far as I know, this article of adornment is never depicted on a divinity, while it is customary on female votaries. In the background between the two figures certain rectangular forms without bases are faintly discernible; they may possibly indicate buildings. (Cf. the small ring from Tiryns, no. 25.) In the intermediate space above these two figures, a celestial body is depicted, a relatively small circle surrounded by radiating rays. Below the entire scene a ground line is indicated, which supports the two figures and the foremost part of the construction.

It is probable that we have here the epiphany of the male god near his sacred enclosure, in the summer season. We should observe the strong parallelism between the exterior depicted in this representation and that in our ring no. 15— a parallelism which is all the closer if we keep in mind that the representation given in no. 15 is made from a positive cast of the ring, while that of no. 20 comes from a galvanoplastic copy of the original engraving, which gives, of course, the negative representation. If we should place our picture of no. 20 face down on no. 15, we would have the principal elements in both representations in the same positions from right to left; that is, the enclosure, the epiphanal image of the male god, and the female votary. In both representations, each of these elements carries the same value.

The differences in the two representations are easily enough explained. Observe that the leaves on the tree in ring no. 15 are small, whereas those in ring no. 20 are fully grown. In no. 15 the lamp within the opening of the enclosure refers to sun magic, a reference which is unnecessary in no. 20, where the sun itself is shown; the sun is strong, and therefore the god is grown great. The open-handed gesture of the god on ring no. 20 represents a command directed to the votary. From the position of his downward-held right hand and the backward-curved object beside it—which could hardly be a loin cloth—we may surmise that he is holding a bow; compare rings nos. 1 and 15.

From our representation we must conclude that the sun, which, though life-quickening in the spring, is death-bringing in the autumn, is connected with the armed male god. From this we are led to the later Apollo, the Sun God with bow and arrows—the sun's beams being the arrows.

Ring no. 21.—A small ring of electron with a sketchy engraving, which comes from Mycenae, is here reproduced after a cast published by Evans, *Palace of Minos*, III, p. 464, fig. 324.

At the extreme left a rocky landscape is depicted. Back to this, a woman is seated on a low stool of peculiar shape. She wears a short skirt, and her upper body is naked. She has rings around her ankles and a bracelet on her right wrist, and her hair above her forehead is adorned with flowers, as on our representation no. 22. She leans slightly forward, her left arm partly extended, elbow on knee and the open hand showing the tips of the thumb and index finger pressed against each other. The right arm is drawn back; it is bent at the elbow, and the hand is seen, with fingers outstretched, at the waist. Standing before her is a youth in a short loin cloth. In his left hand he holds a spear; his right arm, extended toward the woman, is adorned with an armlet at the wrist, and the index finger points directly at the seated figure, the other fingers being clenched. From the gestures it is evident that a "sacra conversazione" is in progress; with Evans, we may view the two figures as the Great Goddess and her male partner. Nilsson wished to secularize the representation (cf. *Minoan-Mycenaean Religion*, p. 303), but the very rendering of such a scene on a gold ring attests sufficiently its sacred character. The most interesting thing here is the sign language: the young god has evidently spoken, and the gesture made by the goddess, of thumb pressed against index finger, is, as Evans has pointed out, a "widespread expedient in sign language for indicating agreement which to the modern Neapolitan still conveys the idea of plighted troth." In their belief that both figures make the same gesture, Evans and Nilsson have unwittingly misinterpreted the representation. The strongly articulated, and here unnaturally large hands, which cross each other at the focal point of the representation, show that conversation is an essential part of it. It is as if the goddess had accepted a promise from the lesser god.

Ring no. 22.—The richest of all the gold signet rings with cult representations belongs to the great treasure discovered by Schliemann, south of the Shaft Grave Circle at Mycenae. It has been dealt with on innumerable occasions, and is here reproduced after a cast published by Tsountas in *Revue Archéologique*, 1900, pl. VIII, 1.

Under a tree with abundant foliage, evidently fruit-laden, a woman, naked to the waist, is seated on the ground. Her lower limbs are clad in a richly adorned flounced skirt. Her left upper arm touches the tree trunk; the arm is bent at the elbow and the hand is placed before her waist. The right arm also is bent at the elbow, and in the extended hand she holds three poppy heads on long stalks. A necklace is about her throat, and flowers are wound in her hair above her forehead. Long plaits of hair also hang down her back. The tree behind her has a strongly grooved trunk (cf. no. 12) which grows from a raised rocky ground. Before her, standing, is another female figure on the same scale, similarly clad from the waist down. Her hair is done in the same way, and she wears two necklaces. Her left arm is extended toward the seated figure, as if she had just presented the poppies. Her right arm is at her side, slightly bent at the elbow. Behind her a similar female figure in a somewhat simpler skirt approaches; she is wearing only one necklace, but her head is also adorned with the same flower-dressed coiffure. She holds a bouquet in her raised left hand, and in her right hand she carries two large iris-like flowers on long stalks.

In order to include as many figures as possible in the representation without overlapping, the artist has depicted two other women, but on a smaller scale. Any belief that they were intentionally foreshortened in perspective and therefore meant to be seen in the background is excluded by the Minoan conceptions of graphic space. I have been unable to find any indication that they are idols, or statuettes, as Herkenrath (*American Journal of Archaeology*, 1937, pp. 411 f.) has suggested. One of them, who appears behind the tree far to the right, is evidently engaged in plucking fruit from it. She wears a flounced skirt, and stands upon a raised section of the ground. Between the seated woman and the large female figure standing before her, the surface is treated in the same manner as under the tree, to represent a rocky terrain. Upon this, a second small female figure is represented. She is dressed in the same fashion as the larger women. She also is presenting flowers, or probably spikes, to the seated one. I cannot agree entirely with Evans that these two smaller figures are the attendants of the goddess, Διόσκουραι, from the parallels to which he refers (cf. *Palace of Minos*, II, pp. 339 ff., figs. 194 *a*, *b*, *c*).

The two parallel crooked lines visible between the last-mentioned figure's head and the spikes in the left hand seem at first to be enigmatical, but their significance becomes clear from similar lines which appear before the small figure farthest to the right and above the forearm of the foremost large standing woman. They also recur to the left of the figure-eight shield, to which we shall return later. In my opinion, these lines represent the ground (cf. no. 12).

Precisely the same sort of irregular lines occur in vase decoration as a complementary ornament, though their character has not been determined despite the evidence of their context. They occur on the group of the so-called Palace Style vases, though, it should be emphasized, only on those with plant motifs. Occasionally a small chevron, representing a plant, occurs on the top of the undulating or wavy line (cf., e.g., *Asine*, pp. 418 f., fig. 272/3; *Athenische Mitteilungen*, 1909, pls. 19:2 f.; the Sakara Alabastron, reproduced by Evans, *Palace of Minos*, II, p. 498, figs. 304 f.). Wace, *Chamber Tombs at Mycenae*, p. 160, merely refers to them as "quirks."

I also find a clue to my interpretation in the small curved line which appears below the shield and above the bouquet held by the woman farthest to the left, as well as in the two points equidistant from the shaft of the double axe, immediately above the left forearm of the foremost standing woman, in which I would see the upper part of a stepped base of the kind that occurs in many places in Crete and also at Mycenae (cf. Wace, *Chamber Tombs at Mycenae*, p. 201). The richly adorned double axe between the standing woman and the seated figure, I cannot believe to be suspended in the air, although this is the general interpretation; rather, I see it as a cult symbol placed inside the sacred area. Likewise, I believe that the figure-eight shield is appended to a standard firmly fixed in the ground; it is to be seen between the heads of the two large standing women. The alternative explanation can only be that it is suspended in space. From above the shield a head protrudes, and from the right side of the upper half of the shield an arm bent upward, with a long, narrow object held in the hand, which is possibly a lance. The lines on the other side of the shield,

Fig. 17. Painted plaster tablet from Mycenae, showing a figure-eight shield.

interpreted by some as flowing locks of hair, indicate, I should say, the ground. Such an extension of the ground is demanded by the six hornless heads which appear around the rim farthest to the left on the representation, and which extend up to the height at which the "quirks" appear. I regard these heads as crania, remains of sacrifices made in the sacred place.

High in the middle of the representation run two undulating parallel lines to denote the sky, and above them a large sun disk, with rays like the spokes of a wheel, and a half moon are depicted. The strangely shaped firmament has already been explained above (p. 26) as dependent upon the fact that a frieze with two zones has served as the model for the representation.

We are evidently within the walls which surround the sacred tree (cf. nos. 15 and 20), and here we obtain a glimpse of how a Mycenaean hypaethral shrine must have appeared. The sacred tree is predominant, and at its foot is seen the epiphany of the Tree Goddess receiving homage. The sacred cult symbols are erected within the walls: we have the double axe on its base, the shield on its standard, half anthropomorphized by a head and an arm, in exactly the same way as on the painted plaster tablet (fig. 17) from Mycenae (cf. Rodenwaldt, "Votivpinax aus Mykenai," in *Athenische Mitteilungen*, 1912, pl. VIII, and pp. 129 ff.; Evans, *Palace of Minos*, III, p. 135, fig. 88). The celestial bodies indicate that the cult place is in the open air, but at the same time suggest that these two planets were connected with the cult.

We should take particular note of the poppy heads which the goddess holds in her hand. They are to be met with elsewhere as hair ornaments together with a στεφάνη; for example, on one of the cylindrical idols from Gazi in Crete, published by Marinatos in *Ephemeris Archaiologike*, 1937, pp. 278 ff. (fig. 10). Marinatos says that they are reproductions of the cultivated species of poppy, *Papaver somniferum*, on pins or hair ornaments; but why can we not consider them to be real flowers, since the female figures on this and other representations are shown with flowers in their hair? *Papaver somniferum* was cultivated as a medicinal plant for the manufacture of opium or oil from the seeds; we have a clear representation of it on a beautiful jug from Phylakopi (cf. Bossert, *Alt-Kreta*, 3d ed., fig. 499). Marinatos concludes that the goddess is meant to be represented by this symbol as "Heilgöttin," Goddess of Healing, but here, it seems to me, his interpretation is too narrow—one need only remember that in classical times the Eleusinian Demeter, goddess of fertility and immortality, is represented with poppies and spikes; for example, on a Boeotian plate (fig. 18) from the 5th century B.C. (cf. Wide, "Eine lokale Gattung Boiotischer Gefässe," in *Athenische Mitteilungen*, 1901, pp. 143 ff., pl. VIII), or on a terra-cotta plaque (cf. Overbeck, *Griechische Kunstmythologie*, II, p. 511, Atlas Taf. XVI, 8).[3]

Fig. 18. Boeotian plate showing Demeter with poppies and spikes.

The representation on this ring has been called a "Minoan Pantheon" by Nilsson, *Minoan-Mycenaean Religion*, p. 348. I hold rather that we have here a graphic picture of the great shrine at Mycenae, which we must evidently seek on the summit of the castle cliff in the immediate neighborhood of the royal palace, where the remains of an archaic temple are still to be found. Here stood the sacred tree of Mycenae, like Athena's olive tree on the Acropolis in

---

[3] In support of my point, cf. the following statement by A. B. Cook, *Zeus*, III, p. 1165: "The poppy has an even greater wealth of tiny seeds. Hence it made for fertility and became the attribute of various mother-goddesses." He gives as examples Demeter, Rhea, Aphrodite, and remarks that poppy heads played their part in the Eleusinian initiation rites (*ibid.*, I, pp. 425 f., also p. 229).

Athens. Here, too, the other cult symbols, the double axe and the shield, would have their natural place.

Ring no. 23.—From the same locality, Mycenae, and from the same find comes a peculiar, extremely worn gold signet ring, here published after a galvanoplastic reproduction pictured by Bossert, *Alt-Kreta*, 3d ed., fig. *392 e*.

Farthest to the left may be seen the contours of what appears to be a large pithos, with three plants or leafy branches rising from it, recalling the Gardens of Adonis in classical times. To the right of this, the representation is divided into two fields by a horizontal row of small rosettes. In each field appear three crania, alternately with and without horns.[4] The three crania without horns are of the same nature as those farthest to the left on the larger gold ring, no. 22. Moreover, at the extreme right on this ring there are indicated, it would seem, some plants.

Keeping in mind the preceding representation—on ring no. 22—we must assume that here, too, we are inside the enclosure of a holy place and that the crania are those of animals offered in sacrifice. They may possibly be attached to the wall, as the rosettes, often met with as wall decoration, may indicate.

Ring no. 24.—The largest gold ring known, up to the present time, comes from the valuable finds made at Tiryns in 1915, and has been published by Karo in *Athenische Mitteilungen*, 1930, pp. 121 ff. It is reproduced here after a plaster cast.

The main representation is pictured as a frieze, the lower part of which is bounded by a straight segmented line, and the upper part by a wavy line. To the right, on our cast, we see a seated goddess in a long tight garment of hide with half-length sleeves and a broad border at the

---

[4] In *Royal Tombs at Dendra*, p. 111, n. 3, I have directed attention to the fact that the so-called crania without horns are of abnormal size in comparison with the ox heads and indicated the similarity to so-called menhir stones; but this is not the place to enter into a closer study of the appearance of such stones in this connection.

hem. She sits on a campstool with a high, slightly curved back. On her head she wears a plate-shaped cap; long hair falls down her back. In her raised right hand she holds a tall, small-based goblet of the kind which has been found, of alabaster, in the Fifth Shaft Grave in Mycenae, and, of silver, in the Royal Tomb of Dendra (cf. *Royal Tombs at Dendra*, p. 51, fig. 30), and which is seen in reproduction

Fig. 19. Scene from the "Campstool Fresco" in Knossos.

on the Campstool Fresco of the Northwest Sanctuary Hall at Knossos (cf. Evans, *Palace of Minos*, IV, p. 390). Evans even speaks of a sacramental class of pedestal goblets. Under the feet of the goddess there is a footstool or cushion with two handles. On the campstool, at the point where the two legs cross, there are three streaks which hitherto have not been explained, but which undoubtedly are gloves (clearly represented on the Campstool Fresco in Knossos: see fig. 19; and compare Evans, *Palace of Minos*, IV, color pl. xxxi, fig. *c*, and p. 388, fig. 323). Behind the stool there is a backward-facing bird, perched on a strangely curved object which recalls most closely a small sacral knot. Underneath appears the corner of a chest with an ornamented half rosette. Before the goddess stands a high, slender object, a column with a capital, presented as though open at the top. It may be a Mycenaean pedestaled lamp or a thymiaterion.

Approaching in parade toward the goddess come four lions, walking on their hind legs, each one holding a beaked jug with a tall slender neck and rounded body and a small foot which rests on the supporting paw. On the back of each lion is, apparently, a hide, possibly covered with a net, and it is held in place by a girdle about the waist, which is visible on the stomach; cf. a wall painting from Mycenae, Nilsson, *Minoan-Mycenaean Religion*, p. 324. The lions thus have the appearance, curiously, of being partly encased by insect wings. Between them are leaved branches, or possibly small cypresses (cf. no. 16), which terminate at their lower ends in double or triple rings which possibly indicate their bases. Over this frieze the space is filled up with small, irregularly dispersed points, apparently stars since among them the sun, a six-spoked wheel, is pictured, and a crescent moon with its horns pointing downward. Furthermore, there are four leaved branches in this field. At the bottom of the entire representation there appears an ornamented architectonic band bounded by straight segmented lines, and, between them, the triglyphic or half-rosette patterns so well known from Minoan-Mycenaean architecture; cf. Evans, *Palace of Minos*, IV, pp. 222 ff. For lack of space, the rosettes at each end are somewhat smaller than those in the middle.

In these festive surroundings, the daemons (the lions) bring to the goddess a libation in the jugs characteristic of the cult vessels; cf. Nilsson, *Minoan-Mycenaean Religion*, pp. 124 f. The raised goblet of the goddess makes it seem probable that this is not a libation in water. In the Minoan-Mycenaean culture, such animal representations have numerous parallels taken over from Egypt and the Orient; cf. Nilsson, *Minoan-Mycenaean Religion*, pp. 319 ff. They are still met with in Hellenistic times; we have, for example, the dancing animals, pigs, rams, donkeys, foxes, and dogs on the veil of Despoina from Lykosura in Arcadia (cf. Dickins' remarks in the *Annual of the British School at Athens*, XIII, pp. 393 f.). It is possible that we have here a scene representing a libation of the first wine of the season, and that the genii are wine daemons. The first offerings of the earth's bounty in the form of wine, oil, and corn were undoubtedly brought, as early as the Minoan period, in strangely matched vessels, the so-called *kernoi*, the same which we meet with in the Eleusinian cult and which persist in a primitive form in the Christian cult in Crete, as shown by Xanthoudidis (cf. the *Annual of the British School at Athens*, XII, pp. 9 f.).

That this representation has a certain connection with the Campstool Frescoes from the Northwest Sanctuary Hall at Knossos—"la Parisienne" belongs there—seems evident to me: we have the campstool, gloves, and peculiar ankle-length dress as common characteristics. The campstool is of Hittite origin (cf. Wrede, *Kriegers Abschied*, pp. 59, 198, n. 184; V. Müller, "Studien zur kretisch-mykenischen Kunst, II," in *Jahrbuch des Deutschen Archäologischen Instituts*, 1922, p. 5). As to the dress itself, Evans (*Palace of Minos*, IV, pp. 397 ff.) has pointed out its Syro-Anatolian origin—he assumes an orientalizing influence through Cyprus. Valentin Müller has emphasized the Oriental influence in different details; cf. *Jahrbuch des Deutschen Archäologischen Instituts*, 1927, pp. 1 ff.

It seems to me not entirely impossible that we have here a type of mystery of a sacramental character; in looking at the daemons on the ring one thinks immediately of the figures masquerading as animals in the later Mithras mysteries.

80 THE PREHISTORIC RELIGION OF GREECE

There follows now a small group of interrelated representations on four gold signet rings, which we shall examine a little more closely.

Ring no. 25.—We begin with the little gold ring, from the treasure find in Tiryns, published by Karo in *Athenische Mitteilungen*, 1930, pp. 121 f. It is reproduced here after a plaster cast.

The ring is badly worn from long use, and many details in the rather hasty engraving are now difficult to determine. It is my opinion that von Salis, *Theseus und Ariadne*, has correctly interpreted the representation as made up of three scenes placed side by side, that is, successive events represented simultaneously.

Scene 1. To the right, on the cast, stand a man and a woman, apparently talking within or in front of a building, which is indicated by two vertical lines to the extreme right; it seems to me incorrect to associate these with the two angled lines which appear to the left of the pair, as one generally seems inclined to do when speaking of an entranceway (see the interpretation of scene 2). The woman is dressed in an ordinary flounced skirt, the man in a loin cloth.

Scene 2. A man and a woman, dressed like the first pair, stand to the left of a pair of angled lines (the horizontals extending to the right from the top of the verticals) which probably depict the doorway of the building at the extreme right. The man, elevated above the woman, bends his right arm at the elbow and holds his left arm along his side. The woman looks up at him. She raises her right arm toward his left arm.

Scene 3. A man and a woman sit facing each other in the cabin of a ship, over which are raised the mast and tackle. Below the ship are four oars, but the rowers are not shown. A dolphin is to be seen at the extreme left, and to the right possibly a cuttlefish. A smaller man, typically wasp-waisted, stands in a characteristic pose facing the cabin. He is probably the steersman, holding the rudder oar which can be seen far to the right under the high stern. A larger man stands in the stern facing the shore as though he were on watch or were exchanging words with the two who are approaching the ship. In the upper part of the representation are a number of strange points and angles which I am compelled—as Karo is—to interpret as buildings in a mountainous terrain.

The interpretation originally proposed by von der Mühl and published by von Salis would have scene 1 represent the first meeting of Theseus and Ariadne; scene 2, the flight; and scene 3, the departure. Others have wished to see in the representation the kidnaping of Helen. Marinatos, *Bulletin de Correspondance Hellénique*, 1933, pp. 227 f., interprets it as the departure of Menelaos and Helen for the Elysian Fields. Others again, Nilsson among them, believe that this is a homecoming scene instead of an embarkation: they point to the large man in the stern, whom they would identify with the man on the shore in both the other scenes.

We have here a ship with its stern toward the land, and perhaps the two principal figures are represented in three different episodes. Let us leave, for the time being, the question of whether this is a departure or a return.

Ring no. 26.—A gold signet ring, found near Candia and probably from the port city of Knossos, is here reproduced after the only available reproduction known to me, a drawing in Evans, *Palace of Minos*, II, p. 250, fig. 147 *b*; IV, p. 953, fig. 923.

To the right we see a ship with its stern toward the shore, and with six rowers, sitting in a row but without marked oars, and in the stern a steersman with a powerful rudder oar. At the bottom of the boat, waves are shown in the form of small angles, and under them three dolphins, as well as some markings to indicate a rocky sea bottom. On the shore stand a man and a woman. The man turns with an inviting gesture in the direction of the vessel, stretching out his left arm toward it, while with his right hand he holds the woman behind him by the wrist. He wears a waist-length shirt and his hair falls down his back. The woman wears a flounced skirt. Behind them, at the extreme left of the engraving, is an elliptical object the upper part of which is like a sharply cut-off slab, probably not a baetyl or sacral tablet (cf., however, ring no. 2), but part of a large pithos with a rim opening. Over the ship appears a tree, and a woman with a relatively short skirt and only one leg. Her right arm is stretched out before her; the left arm is bent downward. Above the outstretched left arm of the man standing on shore is a knoblike mark which, like those before his feet, is probably meant to indicate ground. For this reason I do not interpret, as Evans does, the tree and the woman above the boat "as if in mid-air." I hold that the boat here, as in the representation on ring no. 25, should be thought of as lying in a bay, which the familiar bird's-eye perspective will allow us to imagine.

The representation here seems to give clear indication of a departure. The holy tree on the shore, as well as the idol-like figure with its pile-shaped single leg, as on our representations no. 8 and no. 22, indicates that here we have a sanctuary on the shore, including the holy tree and a bell-shaped idol of the same kind as on ring no. 8. It follows that the goddess is leaving the sanctuary, voluntarily or not, to betake herself over the sea.

Ring no. 27.—This is a gold ring from Mochlos, which unfortunately has been lost; it was published by Seager, *Explorations in the Island of Mochlos,* pp. 89 f., and is reproduced here from his fig. 52.

At the extreme right appears a construction which is apparently the entrance to a holy place, and a piece of the

RINGS AND THE VEGETATION CYCLE 83

high enclosing wall, made of isodomic masonry (as in nos. 15 and 20). Below and in front of the entrance are several round objects which represent the stony shore. To the left appears a craft with its elaborately designed stern toward the land. The forepart of the boat clearly represents a seahorse, a hippocampus. A woman sits in the boat and apparently steadies herself with her right hand against its edge; her left arm is bent at the elbow and she is making what appears to be a gesture of greeting. Under the boat, water is represented by short, comparatively broad vertical lines, perhaps waves. Apparently placed in the boat, but really to be thought of as placed on the shore behind it, stands a tree within an enclosure of rough masonry, and in front of this a construction of like kind.

There are some strange objects above the boat. To the right are two rounded shapes which reminded Seager of a figure-eight shield lying on its side, behind which are indicated some leafless bushes. Marinatos (*Bulletin de Correspondance Hellénique*, 1933, p. 224) recognizes this object as the marine plant, *Scilla maritima*, commonly known as the squib or sea onion. Its broad leaves are shaped like those on our ring, and its large, globular onion is generally visible above the earth where it grows. This plant carries to our own time its supposed magical power of averting evil, and therefore it is hung over house doors on New Year's Day. This virtue was already ascribed to it in classical times, and it was also considered to have a certain therapeutic value (cf. Lucian, *Menippos* 7). It is highly probable that even as early as the Minoan period this plant was held in special regard; the very etymology of the name points to this. One may therefore assume that some manner of religious significance was, at that time, attached to it.

Above these plants there appears something which, very likely, only represents the ground; Marinatos, however, calls it a chrysalis. It is suggestive of the round stones which appear before the entrance to the holy place to the right. Finally, there is a strange object over the head of the woman sitting in the boat, an object which Seager interprets as a "quadruple axe," pictured, like his "shield," in a reclining position.

Even here it is apparent that the woman in the boat is taking her departure from a sanctuary, the construction at the right. The objects in the field over the boat are to be understood as situated on land encircling a bay.

Ring no. 28.—A small gold signet ring from Knossos, published by Evans, *Palace of Minos*, IV, p. 952, fig. 920, is reproduced here after his drawing.

We see a female figure sitting in a boat which has an upturned long-nosed head in the construction of its bow and a triple-branched stern. The woman grasps an oar with both hands. In this representation the waves are roughly depicted in the form of small angles, and perhaps in the lower part a stony shore is indicated.

The last three representations in this group show us a woman—in one of them accompanied by a man—departing in a boat. The holy enclosure, as well as the tree and the reclining symbol, represents in one scene the sanctuary which she leaves; in another this is indicated by a tree and an idol, which we likewise must place on the shore. It is therefore the Great Goddess with whom we are concerned. The analogy from these three representations makes it quite certain that in the first representation also, no. 25, we are to think of a departure, such as has been exhaustively explained by von Salis in both of his treatments of the ring; cf. also "Neue Darstellungen griechischer Sagen," *Sitzungsberichte Heidelberg, phil.-hist. Kl.*, 1936, pp. 38 ff.

In the last four representations we are manifestly concerned with a divine boat of the kind continually met with in Egyptian and Oriental boat-cult scenes, and it is worth noting that the boat in the form it has in our representation no. 25, that is, with the cabin, has no exact counterpart in the Minoan-Mycenaean culture area,[5] but finds it in Egypt—for example, the cult ship of the Sun God from the huge temple in Karnak. It is worth noting especially that the cult boat in Egypt often has a prow which ends in an animal head, for example an antelope head with the head turned inward, like the hippocampus head on the Mochlos ring. Where we find similar boats on Cretan representations we should consider Egyptian influence.

It is especially in the Osiris cult that one meets with this divine boat in Egypt. Osiris is the Egyptian god of fertility, who personifies the annual death and resurrection of vegetation; and in this capacity he became also the one who gave life to the dead and became their tutelary god. In the oldest detailed account of the Osiris cult we possess, dating from the period of the Twelfth Dynasty, an inscription on a stone now preserved in Berlin, there are described the preparations of the Osiris mysteries in Byblos, and we are told, among other things, how the boat of the god, and its cabin, are made. In the myth of Osiris there is a tale of how Isis and her sister Nephtys, with great lamentation, brought the dead body of Osiris in a boat from Byblos back to Egypt. It is highly probable that we have here the boat of the setting sun; the Egyptians thought that the sun traveled in a special boat across the firmament, and a close connection of Osiris with the sun might be assumed. He has, furthermore, been interpreted as a universal god.

The boat cult was also in general vogue in Babylonia, as has been shown by Jastrow, and even there (cf. fig. 20) we can see the double occupants of the boat (as on ring no. 25). And there, too, one can point out a connection between the God of Fertility and the Sun God.[6]

[5] Cf. Marinatos, "La Marine créto-mycénienne," in *Bulletin de Correspondance Hellénique*, 1933, p. 197.
[6] For the cult boat cf. Almgren, *Nordische Felszeichnungen als religiöse Urkunden*, pp. 50 f.

The ship as a means of transportation for the god is naturally native to those countries in which waterways are the most important means of communication, particularly when the figures of the gods are directly related to an island home. We need only recall in this connection the holy ship which stood within the sanctuary of Apollo on Delos, and the peculiar ship's carriage that appears in the cult of Dionysos at the *Dionysia* in Athens. Here also we have a god of fertility in connection with a ship. Nilsson can hardly

Fig. 20. Cylinder seal from Babylonia, showing cult boat with man and woman as occupants.

have been correct in implying that this association only came about because the beginning of seafaring coincides with the time of the great festival of fertility in the spring. The connection between the god or goddess of fertility and the ship can also be apprehended from the fact that divinities of this kind are often, according to legends, born on islands; this applies to Apollo on Delos, Zeus on Crete, Aphrodite on Cyprus or Cythera, and it applies also to the Nordic Nerthus.

We have now examined those gold rings bearing cult representations which we possess from the Minoan-Mycenaean culture area, particularly those about the legitimacy of which there seems to be no doubt. There are, of course, others, but since their authenticity is questionable, on external and internal grounds, our discussion of them may well be postponed until later.

I have attempted to order the cult representations in a particular way, and no doubt my readers have already noted the basic reason for this arrangement. Naturally, reasons can be found for some alteration of the order, for example, no. 2 might be interchanged with no. 7, or no. 6 might be put in place of nos. 3, 4, or 5; but such changes would not disturb the basic view of the material as a whole.

It has long since been agreed that the vegetation cycle must have had great significance in the Cretan religion. Some scholars have maintained from the very beginning that in Minoan religion we have a great nature goddess and her male partner. Scholars have also been tempted to find in the great nature goddess of Crete many characteristics of the great nature goddess of the Near East whom we know by the name of Cybele, later known, in Roman civilization, as *Magna Mater*. Her male partner is therefore naturally comparable with Attis. It is also established that these deities appear aniconically in the tree and in the stone, the baetyl. The evidence for this I shall offer later. But first I must attempt to sum up the testimony offered by the rings we have examined.

CHAPTER THREE

DEATH AND RESURRECTION—OFFERINGS AND FESTIVALS

IN THE preceding chapter I analyzed in some detail the religious representations of those of our gold signet rings concerning the authenticity of which there exists no doubt, and offered a general interpretation of each ring as it occurred in our prearranged series. The rings are our basic texts, so to speak; through them we have attempted to gain some knowledge of the pre-Greek religion. Now I shall enter upon the task of summing up the collective evidence which the representations have offered us thus far.

As you will recall, in those pictographs of our series which fell at the beginning we came upon the act of interment or ritual obsequies, whether a pithos burial (rings nos. 1, 2, 3) or rites performed in a burial enclosure showing a baetyl (no. 4)—which in such representations is to be regarded as a gravestone. An attending factor in such representations is the sorrow of mankind, embodied in the presence of one or more lamenting individuals at the side of tree and stone.

All these representations serve to remind us of inevitable mortality all about us, whether it be the dead child laid in the pithos or the dying vegetation as shown by the falling leaf (no. 2) and the denuded branch (nos. 1, 6). The pain and sorrow of mankind are associated with the bleak world of nature gone dry and desiccate.

There are signs, however, that the divine powers see and hear man's sorrow and lamentation. In that fact is implied a promise that the prayer of the living shall yet be heard. Then the dead shall be quickened and man's hope be renewed, just as the fallow earth comes to life in flower and tree. The eye and the ear (no. 1), the epiphanies of the deity, whether in human form (no. 1) or in a bird's shape

DEATH AND RESURRECTION

(no. 2), the ankh-shaped double axe, and the chrysalis (no. 3)—these speak their unmistakable language. We have noted how man tried to attract the attention of the divinities by shaking the tree (nos. 2, 3, 4), or by conjuring up the heavenly powers through an ecstatic dance (nos. 3, 4, 5), or by gifts (no. 5).

Our first six representations picture the season of winter and the coming spring expressed in budding leaves (nos. 3, 5) or leafy branches (nos. 3, 4). In these the inherent force of nature and of vegetation is potent but quiescent. In no. 6 we have an example of sun magic, the goddess with the mirror; and in no. 20 the operative powers of that magic are shown in the complementary figure of the male god in his reawakened state. The significance of the lamp in the cult—we see it in nos. 15 and 24—is also connected with sympathetic magic: by creating a source of light and heat one influences and impels the great source of light and heat in nature.

With the return of spring, when the lilies on the ground begin to sprout, the goddess of nature manifests herself again to her devoted ones (nos. 7, 8), who piously raise their hands in worship or give expression to their joy by an ecstatic dance, and man receives strength by shaking the blossoming tree (no. 7). In no. 8 the life-giving power of the spring rains, the moisture which quickens and revives the dormant world, is represented by the emergent snake. And in nos. 9, 10, and 11 we see man and beast paying homage to the goddess, who harkens to their prayers. It is at this time that the cult buildings and their holy symbols, the horns of consecration, are decorated with green branches (nos. 12, 13, 14). Thus while every sacred grove is garlanded in green, devotees manifest their adoration by processions to the sacred shrines (nos. 13, 14).

You may recall that the representations on nos. 13 and 14 attracted our special attention. In no. 13 we saw men dressed in skirts; in no. 14, women with but one breast. I suggested that we must assume the males to be the predecessors of Cybele's eunuch priests, the *galli*, and the women to be the earliest representatives of the tribe of Amazons. The sexual mutilations in evidence here are intimately related to the religious worship of fertility. The gift of severed members which the male offers to the deity is designed to strengthen the divine powers in a direct magical way; the transference is easily enough understood, since classical literature gives us precise description of the sacrificial procedure of the galli in this respect. The amputation of the Amazon's breast is an act of exactly the same character, a counterpart to male emasculation. In my view, this practice is the real explanation of the many stories about this peculiarly warlike female group in the literature of antiquity. In later Hellenic thought the Amazons came to signify the growth of unnatural social and religious concepts (cf. Picard, "Die Ephesia von Anatolien," *Eranos-Jahrbuch*, 1938, p. 62). Böckh and Karl Otfried Müller (cf. *Die Dorier*, 2d ed., I, p. 394) were therefore correct, in my opinion, when they identified the Amazons with the hierodules. Indeed, both galli and Amazons, by virtue of a voluntary self-mutilation, have come into a close relationship with the divine powers and thus constitute a caste, if not of priests, at least of specially devoted worshipers of the god. Among us an undeniable parallel exists in monks and nuns; we cannot avoid regarding both these consecrated religious groups in our midst as the direct descendants of these ancient and more crassly consecrated devotees of deity.

In no. 15 the small, armed god manifests himself to the dazzled gaze of the worshiper in proximity to the tree in full bloom and the baetyl. Here the attitude of the woman taken aback by the radiant apparition of the god is similar to well-known representations of like kind in small bronze figures (cf. Bossert, *Alt-Kreta*, 3d ed., nos. 311 *a*, 312, 314 f.). No. 16 shows us a cult scene in a rural milieu by a well, and both the cult building and the baetyl are festively decorated and ornamented with leaves. The gloria radiating from the stone connects it as symbol with the splendor of the sun god.

We have seen spring welcomed by the individual worshiper; yet there is another aspect—which is, I venture to believe, an important result of the present research,—namely, that we can now regard the Cretan bull games as the great official spring festival. Thus, we see a woman athlete, easily recognized by her dress (no. 17), and likewise a male athlete, in his short loin cloth and bound legs (nos. 2, 3, 4, 10, 17), drawing strength for the great and difficult task before them by grasping or shaking the holy tree (no. 17). It is primarily the representation of the women athletes which lends certainty to our conclusions in this respect; we could not be certain if male athletes only were represented, because the Minoan puttees or leggings were worn not only by male athletes, but also by warriors, for example, by the officer on the Hagia Triada cup. We may even be justified in assuming such gear for a person moving about on the ground, as on no. 10 (cf. Evans, *Palace of Minos*, II, p. 728, and the examples given there). The apparel of the male athletes consisted of a belt with a loin cloth of a special narrow kind (cf. Evans, *Palace of Minos*, II, p. 752).

The same symbols that are constantly met with in representations of the bull games, we see used also as signs of a ritualistic character, the figure-eight shield (no. 18) and the sacral knots (no. 19) in an unmistakable cult connection in our representation no. 3. Nilsson, as I have previously noted, denies the sacral significance of both shield and knot. In my opinion, they are symbols whereby the men of that time gave expression to an entire complex of meaning. We should bear in mind that the oldest scripts were purely pictographic, that people of that prehistoric era were accustomed to see their thoughts and ideas generally rendered through the picture or ideogram, and were therefore given to thinking through imagery to a degree unknown and unnecessary to us.

The figure-eight shield is the symbol of divine protection. It is to be seen on a fragmentary clay seal from the "Little Palace" at Knossos, in an environment similar to that on our representation no. 18 (cf. Evans, *Palace of Minos*, III, p. 316). Amulet beads in the shape of such shields are often found. In my opinion, moreover, whenever the shield is displayed inside an enclosure in connection with a tomb (as in no. 4), it is so used to avert evil. Its more obvious significance derives from its representation, real or pictured, on the walls of palaces; examples are to be seen both in Knossos and in Tiryns (cf. Evans, *Palace of Minos*, III, pp. 301, ff.). With the Psalmist's words in mind, "the Lord is our defense" (Ps. 89:18), or "our shield is of the Lord," we can understand the anthropomorphic shape of the shield on ring no. 22. Here the shield within the great sanctuary is to be considered in its larger, more authoritative function of guarding the state against destruction. Gardner in his study, "Palladia from Mycenae," *Journal of Hellenic Studies*, 1893, pp. 21 ff., has given us good reasons for accepting the connection between such an image of the shield as is to be seen on our ring no. 22 with the later palladium. To this Evans adds the Roman *ancilia* (cf. *Palace of Minos*, II, p. 52). A reminiscence of the early symbolism of the shield may perhaps be found in the story of the armed Kouretes who guarded the Zeus-child, clashing their shields and swords in a dance around him.

The sacred knot is another symbol of a similar kind. It indicates that the object to which it is appended is "connected with" the divinity—observe that our language still teems with such obsolete images. The magical virtues of the knot depend upon this. And thus, when we sometimes hear that it is forbidden to wear knots when one approaches the divine, it is as much as to say that one must be free from all earthly ties on such an occasion.

When female votaries wear the knot—the goddess is never shown wearing it—at the nape of their necks (nos. 15, 20), their relation and office to the divinity is made plain. Just so, whenever we see the knot represented at the bull games (no. 19), or under certain other circumstances (cf. Evans, *Palace of Minos*, I, p. 430), a religious relationship is thereby established in scene or object. The occult significance of knots is still widespread. And let me remind you that when Alexander the Great cut the Gordian knot he thereby severed the connection which existed between the temple and its protective deity.

For Nilsson the bull pictured in Cretan religious observances is without cult significance except as a beast of sacrifice. It is true that the sacrifice of the bull in the whole Aegean sphere falls within the frame of worship of "Mother Earth." Nevertheless, Malten had previously established its intimate connection with cult, basing his interpretation on the significance that the bull had in both cult and religion in the entire Near East (cf. "Der Stier in Kult und mythischem Bild," *Archäologisches Jahrbuch*, 1928, pp. 90 ff.). On the strength of my interpretations of scenes such as are pictured on rings nos. 18 and 19, I contend that we have here conclusive evidence for the correctness of Malten's theory. The Great Beast of Heaven and of Fertility must have played an important role, especially at the great spring festival. The bull and the ram had, at an early period, been transposed to the constellation which indicates the coming of spring. Our representations exhibit the reason why. The bull on our rings is shown ithyphallically, that is, as a potent image of the reproductive force. He represents virility and fertility in nature—from an observation which primitive man assuredly made in the first stages of his domestication of animals such as cattle and goats. A female divinity with a bull was still adored in classical times at Colophon (cf. Picard, *Éphèse et Claros*, p. 509). And as Malten has correctly pointed out, there is a further link: the god represented in the figure of a bull is a universal

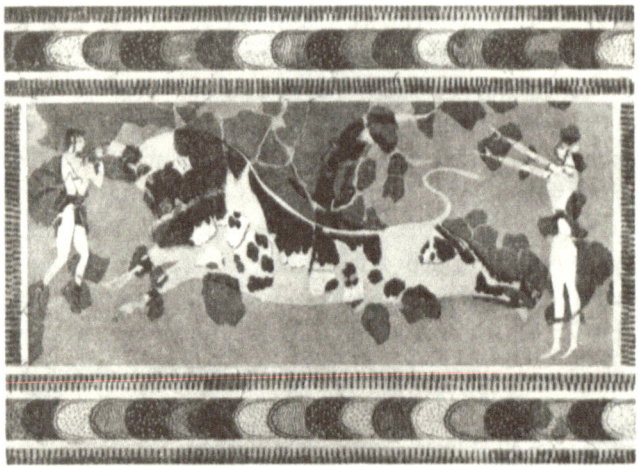

Fig. 21. Fresco from Knossos, showing the somersault performed at a bull game.

God of Fertility and Heaven; Zeus is his counterpart in Greek mythology and often takes on the form of a bull, and Dionysos also is closely allied to this animal in his role of bull god, Zagreus.

We can deal but briefly with the bull games. There have been found, especially in Knossos, many taurine representations, either painted or in stucco reliefs, the majority of which depict scenes from the bull games. In connection with his treatment of the Toreador Frescoes (cf. *Palace of Minos*, III, pp. 203 ff.), Evans has compiled from seals and other such small objects a large amount of illustrative material, to which still more can easily be added. It seems possible to distinguish three main phases in the bull games. The athletes who appear in them, both male and female, are easily distinguished on the frescoes by their skin color: the men are dark and the women fair (fig. 21). This is a conventional way of depicting differences in sex, met with in Egypt and elsewhere, and still in use in the black-figured vase painting of the sixth century B.C. in Greece.

The scene most frequently represented shows an athlete grasping the lowered horns of the charging bull in order to swing himself up and over its back when the animal throws up its head, as on the fresco from Knossos (cf. Evans, *Palace of Minos*, III, p. 212, fig. 144). The athlete's aim is to execute—bracing hand and arms against the bull's back or flanks in the leap—a full somersault, so as to land on his feet in the arena, thereby completing a circle in the air; observe ring no. 18. Other representations show the athlete in another variation of the dangerous leap; using the animal's horns as a lever, he leaps to the back of the rushing bull and thence down to the arena floor again. We have a small bronze group published by Evans showing this (cf. *Palace of Minos*, III, pp. 220 ff., fig. 155).

Evans consulted a celebrated torero concerning these acrobatic feats, and was informed that no bullfighter nowadays would dare attempt to grip the horns of a charging bull for the purpose of gaining momentum for a vault to the animal's back. With the bull rushing toward him, he could not manage a proper balance for the feat; and even were such a leap possible, the athlete would land on the ground behind the bull, not on his back. However this may be, the representations of bull vaulting are so numerous and so specific that one can only say that the ancient athletes excelled in a feat which modern champions consider impossible. That it was an exceedingly perilous feat is attested by many of the representations, which show the athlete either spitted on the horns of the bull or trapped on the ground under his hoofs (no. 19).

Another phase of these games is apparently revealed in representations which show a contestant who grasps the bull's horns and swings himself over from one side to the other (fig. 22). He is usually shown as doing this with one hand only. The bull is represented as standing, or, in one

Fig. 22. Seal stone showing an athlete swinging himself over the bull from one side to the other.

illustration, as lying down, and the athlete's feat is obviously a less dangerous form of the backward somersault.

The climactic feat of these old Cretan bullfights, and one in which the athletes were rarely successful, is pictured on a number of seal stones. On these the principal, in a half-kneeling position, and obviously by summoning every ounce of his strength, twists and breaks the neck of the bull (fig. 23). Grasping the bull's muzzle with one hand, and one of the horns with the other, he bends the animal's head with a sharp, violent movement. Pliny refers to such a manner of killing bulls. The American cowboy was proficient in this practice in early days, and the more refined version of "bulldogging" is still exhibited annually at the western rodeos. Parenthetically, we may note that one seal stone shows an athlete shouldering the vanquished bull on high, to remind us of the Heraklean legend of that champion bearing the Cretan bull home to Mycenae.

These games, intimately associated with the vegetation cult, are possibly connected with other games, *agones*, as shown on the large steatite rhyton from Hagia Triada. It has been customary to connect the origin of the agones with

Fig. 23. Seal stones showing the climactic scene of the bull games.

"Leichenspiele" or "Funeral games"; it is my opinion that these in turn go back to purely religious games of the kind we meet with here, which are closely connected with fertility rites. Such rites, as we know, have much in common with funeral rites.

The bull games were possibly unknown originally to the Greek mainland; and this need not surprise us when we consider the difference of race. The Greek religion of the mainland was no doubt touched by Minoan influence in gradual stages—though its indigenous features are still difficult to determine with exactitude. That the Cretan bull games are reflected in the saga of Theseus is now generally assumed. And that the sacrifice of freemen originally offered to the bull underwent a change with time, prisoners of war being substituted, is a plausible conclusion, to judge from related practice in other instances.

King Minos in Knossos had forced the submission of Athens and required the Athenians every ninth year to send seven noble youths and seven maidens to Crete, where they were imprisoned in the Labyrinth as an offering to Minotaur, the bull of Minos. As the story runs, the third time this sorrowful tribute was about to depart, the young prince Theseus offered to go along. The beautiful Cretan princess, Ariadne, fell in love with Theseus, and with her help he was enabled to gain entrance to the monster; he killed it, and, following Ariadne's thread through the tortuous passages of the Labyrinth, emerged again to the waiting youths and girls who were to have been sacrificial victims. He conducted them unharmed to their homes, accompanied by Ariadne.

One thinks of these Athenian youths and maidens when one sees the male and female athletes pictured in the representations of the bull games, and at the scene in which the athlete breaks the neck of the bull one recalls Theseus to mind. Minotaur—half human and half beast—is, in my opinion, to be conceived simply as the priest-king, Minos—this is not a proper name, but a title, like that of Pharoah in Egypt—enveloped in the ritual cult dress, the bull's hide, and officiating at the sacrifice in honor of the beast.

Let us now return to our representations. No. 20 shows that summer has come: the sun shines in all its strength and the tree in full foliage lifts its shading branches over the enclosure. Before it stands the male god, large and strong, and he turns in speech to the votary. The gesture reminds us of the "sacra conversazione" in no. 21.

Representation no. 22 shows full summer; the worshipers, with poppy heads, spikes, and flowers, approach the goddess seated under the tree. As we have noted earlier, we find ourselves here within the wall which surrounds the sanctuary of the goddess; the holy tree and the sacred symbols—the double axe and the shield—have their place here, as well as the heads of the animals sacrificed in her honor. We see the heads also on representation no. 23, and in such a position that we are inclined to conceive of them as attached to the walls of the enclosure. The sun and the moon in the sky have undoubtedly something to do with the divinities: the moon with the Great Goddess (cf. below, p. 136), judging by the myths which will be treated later, the sun, as already emphasized, with the male god. There is also the first suggestion, in no. 23, in the plants sprouting from a vessel, of the "Gardens of Adonis" of later days.

No. 24 we interpreted as a first offering of wine to the Great Goddess because of the stemmed goblet she holds in her hand; it is possibly a sacramental act, and can scarcely be merely rain magic, as has most often been proposed. Even here we have the green branches and the cypresslike trees, as well as the sun (but without aureole) and the moon in a peculiar aspect with both horns pointing downward.

When the vegatational god, whom I prefer to regard as an agricultural deity, like Triptolemos of later days, is buried, the universal Goddess of Fertility disappears over the sea, only to return when vegetation is reborn. On our representations nos. 25 to 28 we have scenes illustrative of this event. The goddess departs from her island. She takes her boat out from the sanctuary that we see in no. 27, where indeed the prone axe signifies that the god is dead. In the double enclosure shown on this ring we see, in the higher one, the tree; in the smaller one beside it the baetyl probably had its place. In representations nos. 25 and 26 the goddess is apparently being guided on her journey by a male partner, who has come to fetch her; around this theme the legends of Theseus and Ariadne and of Paris and Helen have been elaborated. With this journey over the water I am inclined to associate certain practices later obtaining, in which the cult statue of the goddess was annually submerged under the water, an act that developed into a special rite of purification.

We have seen different kinds of cult places: enclosures with the holy tree and the stone (nos. 4, 5, 7, 10, 17, 27), tripartite altarlike cult constructions (nos. 5, 12, 13, 14), actual *temenoi* with surrounding high walls (nos. 15, 20, 27), and cult representations in a free landscape, in a meadow (no. 8), or by a well (no. 16).

Especially noteworthy are the small one-legged idols on rings nos. 8 and 26. They are related to the well-known bell-shaped idols. Our rings show that Marinatos can hardly be correct in dating all such idols to the Late Minoan III period (cf. *Ephemeris Archaiologike*, 1937, p. 289).[1] The dating to Late Minoan I of the idol from Prinia by Evans (cf. *Palace of Minos*, IV, pp. 160 f., n. 4) seems to me quite reasonable, the more so because we see in figures like those in question a further development, in my opinion, of the cylindrical rhyta in female shape, known from Mochlos, Mallia, and other places, which can be traced back to Early Minoan III (cf. Nilsson, *Minoan-Mycenaean Religion*, p. 122).

In summary, we may gather something like the following outline from the representations on our gold rings. We are given a vegetation cycle which is divided into the various seasons of the year (winter, spring, summer, harvest, and fall), each with its special rites, private cult practices, and large official festivals; and this picture will be strengthened and more sharply defined if we view the cycle in the light of similar religious practices from neighboring culture areas. But first a few words about several other gold rings which

---

[1] The so-called "Lord from Asine," published by me, *Asine*, p. 308, fig. 211, is to be connected with these figures. I have now come to the opinion, in agreement with Evans (cf. *Palace of Minos*, IV, p. 756), that it is female, partly because of the white paint, which was a feminine convention, and partly because of the striking similarity with female idol no. 1 from Gazi (cf. Marinatos in *Ephemeris Archaiologike*, 1937, pp. 278 ff.)—the figure from Asine differing in having plastic plaits of hair.

some of you may possibly have missed in our discussion hitherto.

For our present purpose we may disregard the "Ring of Nestor" and the treasure from Thisbe, partly because of their representations and partly because of the well-grounded doubts of their authenticity; one could easily pile up additional arguments to prove their lack of authenticity, but it would lead us away from our present purpose. We may likewise dismiss because of its representation the so-called "Minotaur Ring" found in the American excavations in Athens and published by Shear (cf. *American Journal of Archaeology*, 1933, p. 540, fig. 1). On this ring I do not see Minotaur and the Athenian maidens, but a predecessor to Hermes ψυχοπομπός, "the leader of souls," who, staff in hand, conducts the imprisoned dead away from this world to the kingdom of the dead. Likewise we need not dwell on a series of other gold rings which represent sphinxes or griffins—I shall merely note them. Among these, one ring from Mycenae displays a seated goddess facing a chained griffin (cf. Bossert, *Alt-Kreta*, 3d ed., fig. 399 *e*); this seems to me to be related to the myth of the underworld—compare the so-called "harpies" on the sarcophagi and grave monuments, especially from Asia Minor. Another ring, also from Mycenae, shows two griffins in a heraldic scheme (cf. *ibid.*, figs. 395 f.). We possess several with representations of sphinxes (cf. *ibid.*, figs. 391 *c*, 395 *b*, both from Mycenae, and another from Rhodes, cf. Maiuri, *Annuario della Reale Scuola Archaeologica di Athene*,VI–VII), which are linked to a large group of rings of purely heraldic character. None of these rings is related to our present purpose or subject matter, the Vegetation Cycle, and we may therefore omit them from our discussion.

But to the so-called "Ring of Minos," no. 29 of our reproductions, published by Evans in *Palace of Minos*, IV, pp. 947 f., we must give some attention. Evans himself reports fully on the rather peculiar provenance of the ring; it is therefore not necessary for us to detail it. It was *not* found in the course of an excavation, but was brought to Evans by a peasant, whose son, according to report, had come upon it accidentally.

The representation is one of the fullest to be met with on Minoan gold rings. It actually divides itself into three parts, which I have indicated on the reproduction of the ring given here. In the lower part, we have in the main a copy of the Mochlos ring, our no. 27; the goddess is depicted standing, oar in hand, in a boat the forward part of which is in the form of a sea horse, and the stern, of a tripartite fish's tail. In the boat are two cult buildings, of unequal height, both bearing horns of consecration. The background is a pattern apparently meant to suggest waves. As we stated earlier, when discussing ring no. 27, the two cult constructions on the Mochlos ring are to be thought of as situated on the shore. Through a misunderstanding of the engraver's meaning, they have here been placed in the boat, and the tree has been replaced with horns of consecration. As a prototype for the waves I am inclined to refer to a fragmentary gold ring from Phaistos, published in *Monumenti antichi*, XIV, p. 592, fig. 53. A similar pattern is often found on Mycenaean vases in a variation of the so-called scale pattern.

The representation in the oval to the right we find again on the Phaistos ring, our no. 2, picturing a woman who bends down the trunk of a tree growing in a sacral enclosure. Even on our ring the woman is unusually well formed, and this effect is enhanced by the loin cloth. One leg is placed on a considerably higher plane than the other. The twist of the body is, to be sure, different from that seen on the "Ring of Minos," and likewise the position of the arms, but compare that figure with the dancing woman on our representation no. 3. Even here, the artist of the "Ring of Minos" has been guilty of a serious error. He permits the holy tree to grow from the top of an altar-like building, instead of from the enclosure as we have it in our representation no. 2, and as it is found, furthermore, on several other gold rings we have analyzed. The large stones which are placed at the base of the altar, and for that matter, also, as fillings between the three ovals on the "Ring of Minos," go back evidently to the misconceived pithos on the Phaistos ring, no. 2.

There remains the upper left representation of this ring. The seated Great Goddess, supported against the altar with the horns of consecration, by the coquettish movement of her arms reminds us immediately of the goddess seated by the column on the Phaistos ring, no. 9, where the arm movements are explained as a greeting to the votary and the worshiping animal. The hovering two-legged female figure above her evidently has some connection with the small idol on our representation no. 8, the ring from the Isopata grave, where the idol is characterized as such by a single support, which may be thought of as stuck down in the ground.

And finally, with respect to the male figure who, in an almost kneeling position, stretches up his left arm to the branches of the tree and in his bent right hand seems to hold an oil flask, we are immediately reminded of our representation no. 3 from the Isopata grave.

Once we point out these synthetic elements in the ring, it seems unnecessary to say that the scenes reproduced here are not, as a unit, easy to fit into the vegetation cycle which we have been able to elicit from the definitely authentic representations. The person who made this ring was assuredly a skilled artist. In some details he was able to approximate the Minoan style, and he had some familiarity with cult representations on other rings; but apparently he had not mastered that knowledge to the point of being able to create a trustworthy picture in every respect. Consequently the slips he made, as pointed out here, betray him mercilessly. In the copying of a representation one always runs the danger of misinterpretation, as Robert (*Archäologische Hermeneutik*, pp. 1 f.) emphasizes so strongly—especially in the matter of detail, when one does not understand the meaning of what is represented.

We have now reached the point in our study where the contributive light shed by contemporary religious practices of other lands and neighboring culture areas, whether in Asia Minor, Syria, or Egypt, can be helpful to a more searching and intimate view of our subject. Indeed, the comparison should help to strengthen and clarify our ideas and interpretations of those fundamental elements of the Vegetation Cycle of the pre-Greek religion which we are trying to establish.

CHAPTER FOUR

MINOAN-MYCENAEAN RELIGION COMPARED WITH THE RELIGIONS OF ASIA MINOR, SYRIA, BABYLONIA, AND EGYPT

As Evans pointed out long ago, the goddess on the mountaintop, flanked by lions, as seen on seal impressions from Knossos, closely resembles the lion goddess of Asia Minor, Μήτηρ ὀρεία, Πότνια θηρῶν. This gives us occasion to turn first toward Asia Minor, since we must discover what, if any, vegetation cults existed in these areas adjacent to Greece.

The great nature goddess of Asia Minor is known by the name of Cybele or Cybebe. Her name may possibly have been given a satisfying etymological explanation by Suidas through his gloss *s.v.* Κυβηλίσαι—κύβηλις γὰρ ὁ πέλεκυς (cf. Wace, *Chamber Tombs at Mycenae*, pp. 200 f.). If so, she is to be regarded as the female counterpart to Zeus Labrandeus, and the axe as her holy symbol. Her country of origin was Phrygia, especially the area about Pessinus, to which are tied the legends of Cybele—her cult was undoubtedly older than the Thraco-Phrygian influx. The mother sanctuary was established in Pessinus, whence the cult of the goddess and her sphere of authority found gradual extension, like those of other Oriental divinities from other centers. The divine power of Cybele was embodied in a baetyl, which was to be found in Pessinus from earliest times until, in 205/4 B.C., it was removed to Rome. It was apparently a meteor fragment, small, uncut, and black in color (cf. Arnobius, *Adv. nationes* VII, 49). Sacred stones as places of habitation for supernatural powers have in general been very common in Asia Minor (cf. de Visser, *Die nicht menschengestaltigen Götter der Griechen*, pp. 56 ff.), as well as in Semitic culture areas; cf., for example, the "Black Stone" in the Kaaba at Mecca.

Cybele must originally have been a sort of universal divinity, like Jahve among his people and the local Baals for their worshipers. Cybele was the mother of all other gods, Μήτηρ θεῶν, *Mater deum*, and thus she was denoted as mother through lallation by the words *ma, nanna,* or *amma.* She has created, and she maintains, all life. The eventual designation Μεγάλη, or *Magna*, expresses her sublimity. Her all-inclusive significance is associated undoubtedly with primitive ideas which made no clear distinction as between fertilization and birth and which included the notion of the mother as the divine creator of all life. A later, more searching period, the thought of which on this matter grew more distinct, joined the male principle to the female; and with Cybele there are sometimes still to be found in classical times on Near Eastern soil closely related divinities in androgynous form. Thus it was held that the Great Mother conceived by a special potency, namely, by virtue of male genital parts, gifts to her, in which the reproductive power was embodied. In similar cults the Greeks were content with exhibiting phallic images; for example, in the festivals *Thesmophoria* and *Dionysia*. But in the great Spring Festival of Cybele there were actually consecrated to her the shorn genitals of her priests. These objects, occult and potent, were then buried in the ground so that their life-giving force should reanimate the earth.

On the last day of the great Spring Festival the symbol of the goddess was "baptized" at Pessinus, probably in the Gallos River, on the shore of which the festival took place. A similar practice known in other regions, both in Asia Minor and elsewhere, is interpreted either as rain magic or as a rite of lustration.

Cybele thus has the characteristics of the widely known "Mother Earth." She makes the fields fertile, since according to the cult saga the fruits of the field have been disseminated over the earth from her homeland. Even up to the time of Roman coinage the goddess is portrayed with branches in her hands, along with her high priest bearing the axe.

There were certain rites connected with the worship of the goddess of vegetation with which a male vegetation god was associated. In Phrygia, and later on in Rome, a perennially verdant tree—a pine or a fir—in which the creative power of nature seemed to exist even during the winter was decorated at the Spring Festival with woolen bindings and with violets and the first flowers of spring. On the tree was hung an image of a youth, an embodiment in human form of that power which really dwelt within the tree. It was buried to the accompaniment of loud lamentations. After three days it was unearthed and preserved until the following year, when it was burned. With the spirit of vegetation, which was buried as dead and thereafter awakened, Nature herself awakens to new life. This god, with the lall-name Attis (= father) was placed by the side of the Great Mother. He was thus put on a par with the priest whose genitals had fertilized the "Mother" and who also bore the name Attis.

Now the sacred grotto in which the grave of Attis, decorated with a phallos after the Phrygian custom, had its place, was to be found in Pessinus; whence the indigenous saga of Attis is derived, as is related by Pausanias (vii, 17, 9 ff.) and, with some slight variation in detail, by Arnobius (*Adv. nationes* V, 5 ff.). Pausanias gives the following account. From the seed of Zeus, which floated down to the earth while he slept, arose a hermaphroditic being by the name of Agdistis—a surname of Cybele after the mountain Agdos, which is near Pessinus. (Parenthetically, I would here remind my readers that the saga names the same locale for the episode involving Deukalion and Pyrrha, who created men from stones.) The gods captured Agdistis and deprived him of his male character. From the shorn organ there grew forth an almond tree. The daughter of the river god Sangarios picked its fruit and hid it in her bosom. She then conceived and gave birth to a boy, Attis, who was left to die but was saved from that fate and cared for by a goat. Agdistis fell in love with the beautiful youth, but the boy's relatives sent him to Pessinus to espouse the king's daughter. While the wedding was being celebrated, Agdistis appeared and drove Attis and the king insane to the degree that they ravished themselves of their virility. Agdistis regretted the deed and bade Zeus keep the marvelous body of Attis from decay.

Arnobius narrates this version. Zeus, who wished to possess Cybele, copulated with the rock instead, and thus the terrible double-sexed Agdistis was born, whom Dionysos made drunk and then deprived of his virility. From the blood that was shed, there grew forth a pomegranate tree. Nana, the daughter of Sangarios, became pregnant from eating of its fruit and gave birth to Attis. Cybele and Agdistis both wished to lie with him, although King Midas desired to marry him to his daughter. They were all thrown into a frenzy by the jealous Agdistis. Attis and his companions ravished themselves of their virility, the bride killed herself, and their blood nurtured violets and an almond tree. Zeus granted the prayer of Agdistis that the body of Attis should not decay, that his hair should continue to grow, and that his little finger should move constantly. In memory of this, Agdistis founded the annual festival cult of Attis at Pessinus.

According to Plutarch, *De Iside et Osiride*, 69, two festivals were celebrated yearly in honor of Attis; one in the fall, when the god retired to sleep, and the other in the spring, when he awaked again. Other writers mention only one festival, namely, in the spring. According to Diodoros (III, 59, 7), Apollo had commanded the Phrygians to bury the body of Attis and to worship Cybele as a divinity. This ceremony the Phrygians performed even in the time of Diodoros. Hepding, *Attis, Seine Mythen und sein Kult*, p. 131, maintains that in fulfillment of this command there was instituted a rite in imitation of the preparing of the dead for burial, a *prothesis*, that is, at which the dead was mourned with great lamentation, cries of distress, and wild beating of the breast, indeed even self-mutilation. At the festival of Adonis the Syrians gave expression to their sorrow over the early death of the youth, in exactly the same way as described, among others, by Plutarch, *Alcibiades* XVIII. In rural regions of Greece today one can see similar scenes at the Easter Festival. The burial of the Attis image, it seems quite certain, took place on the following day. Shortly thereafter the priests gave assurance, according to what Julius Firmicus Maternus, *De errore profanarum religionum* III, reports, that Attis was again risen. This resurrection was celebrated with great joy and jubilation; the festival of Adonis in Byblos, which we shall touch on presently, supplies us with an excellent parallel. This Spring Festival was celebrated, as Buresch (*Aus Lydien*, pp. 70 f.) has shown, in the month of Artemisios, that is, in March-April.

These comparatively late cult legends and cult practices make possible certain conclusions regarding the basic concepts involved. From various temples in Asia Minor, for example in Ephesus, according to Strabo (XIV, 641 c), and in Stratonikeia (cf. *Corpus Inscriptionum Graecarum*, no. 2715) come references to castrated priests. The galli associated with the cults of Cybele and Attis are, however, as indicated earlier, hardly to be understood as genuine clergy. The kind of self-mutilation with which we are here concerned is undoubtedly very old in Near Eastern religions; certainly the custom goes back to pre-Phrygian times. Attis is an indigenous god and his story is nothing more than an etiological explanation for the cult practice out of which it grew. It is certainly incorrect to trace the rites from the myth, as was done of old; on the contrary, the myth grew out of the rites.[1] For acceptance into the corps of the galli, castration was an inflexible requirement. By this act the gallus was consecrated to the great nature goddess and was thereafter considered her slave. After a primitive custom, a sharp stone, according to the witnesses of antiquity, was used for the operation. The genitals were subsequently buried.

In order to resemble the goddess to whom they had consecrated themselves, the galli wore female attire, including an ankle-length skirt of variegated colors. On their heads they wore a tiara with falling flaps, or a miter. Their long, unclipped hair was smeared with salves and bound up. They were adorned, also, with necklaces and rings. Wild orgiastic dances were included in the practices of the cult.

There was an inclination among early scholars to assume a Semitic influence in these elements; but it has been shown that, on the contrary, it is more probable that the North Syrian cults were exposed to a Hittite–Asia Minor influence, as Cumont maintains in his article, "Gallos" (cf. Pauly-Wissowa, *Real-Encyclopädie*, VII, p. 679). Be that as it may, the practice as we find it in Syria varies very little from that of Phrygia. Even there, the sacrifice took place at the great Spring Festival, at which, as related by Lucian, *De dea Syria*, 49–52, galli as well as many other hierodules functioned. According to Lucian, the orgies took place outside the temple, into which the galli could not enter. To the accompaniment of deafening music and loud cries they lacerated their own arms and scourged one another's backs. Many who had come only as spectators were so gripped by the frenzy that they tore their clothes from their bodies and, with loud shouts, threw themselves into the crowd of those who were carried away to excess,

---

[1] For ethnological parallels cf. Frazer, *The Golden Bough*, IV, 1, pp. 270 f.

and, seizing a sword designed for that purpose, castrated themselves. Then they ran through the city with the shorn member, and from the house into which they cast it they were given female dress and female adornments. Should any die from the mutilation, their comrades bore the bodies to a place outside the city, and over the bodies was heaped a pile of stones. Thus they were abandoned. Note that they were not buried in the earth. The bearers themselves were unclean for seven days and were kept away from the sacred rites.

The interpretation which the Attis myth had already received in Porphyrius—it is still the explanation given it by modern science—is expressed in the following words of Cumont: "Attis personnifie probablement la végétation, brûlée par les ardeurs de l'été avant d'avoir atteint sa maturité, et qui durant l'hiver paraît s'affaiblir et pour ainsi dire perdre sa virilité, puis mourir, pour renaître au printemps avec un nouvel éclat" ("Notice sur un Attis funéraire," *Extrait du Bulletin de l'Institut Archéologique Liégeois*, 1901, p. 5).

Rapp in his article on Cybele sums up the Agdistis-Attis myth as follows: "Agdistis, die Erdmutter, vereinigt ..., um alles Leben in der Natur aus eigner Kraftfülle hervorbringen zu können, die Zeugungskraft beider Geschlechter, die sich jedoch alsbald wieder differenzieren.... Aus der Einheit der Lebenskraft als Mutter (Kybele) geht das vegetative Leben als Sohn (Attis) hervor.... Die Mutter Erde liebt den aus ihrem Schoss entsprungenen Blütenflor.... Die anfangs unbegrenzte Zeugungskraft erfährt eine plötzliche Hemmung im Absterben der Vegetation: Attis entmannt sich" (in Roscher, *Mythologisches Lexikon*, II, p. 1648).

If we have examined in some detail the vegetation religion with special reference to aspects of its practice in Asia Minor, we have only done so because there are many signs which point to an especially intimate connection between it and that related practice which is represented on our rings. We shall here touch only briefly on one other myth complex which has earlier received a false interpretation because it has never been considered in relation to pre-Greek religion, namely, the concept of the Amazons. According to the unanimous tradition of antiquity, the Amazons belong to Asia Minor, and there has even been a disposition to identify them with the Hittites (cf. Leonhard, *Hettiter und Amazonen*). That this is out of the question need not be demonstrated at this time.

The transparent etymology tells us that this female group was characterized by the absence of both breasts or at least the right one (Diodoros II, 45, 3; Justinus II, 4, 11)—the avowed reason being that the breasts would not then hinder the use of the bow. But as I see it, theirs is an act of self-mutilation of a kind closely comparable to that of the galli. The woman who consecrated herself to the Great Goddess wished to fortify the divine power by the offer she brought, and this involves an obvious and simple magical procedure. Rightly enough, as we previously noted, both Böckh and Otfried Müller have viewed these Amazons as hierodules of the same kind as the galli, worshipers consecrated to the goddess. That later Greek legend transforms them into a tribe among which no men were tolerated is, undoubtedly, as Otfried Müller emphasizes, the result of "der Anblick der ungeheuren Heerden von Tempeldienerinnen, Hierodulen, wie sie in Asiatischen Tempeln sich vorfanden" (cf. *Die Dorier*, 2d ed., p. 394), and of the exclusively dominating position assumed by the goddess. The allusions to an original matriarchy, such as Eduard Meyer, *Geschichte des Altertums*, 3d ed., I, 1, pp. 23 f., asserts that he has found in the sagas, are connected with the ascendancy of the female divinity. We shall return to the Amazons again in a later connection.

Let us now consider the divinities comparable to Cybele and Attis in Syria and Egypt. We can do so, briefly, by referring to Frazer, "Adonis," "Attis," "Osiris," in *The Golden Bough*, IV. But first a word about some later researches.

Until recently we have had only late sources for our knowledge of the comparable deities in Syria, but now, thanks to the exceedingly significant finds of new inscriptions in Ras Shamrah, made available and interpreted in the main by the learned Frenchman, Virolleaud, in his articles in the review *Syria*, we have documentation from the fourteenth or fifteenth centuries B.C. From the evidences of conservatism which the religious ideas expressed in these inscriptions show, we may have some justification for drawing analogous conclusions even where such old sources are lacking.

The most animated and impressive figure in these mythological accounts is a goddess, sometimes called Astart, that is, Astarte, but most often Anat—known earlier in Egypt through building inscriptions from the 18th and 19th Dynasties, and apparently introduced there by the Hyksos. In Ras Shamrah this goddess always appears in the company of a god, sometimes brother, sometimes husband, who is designated as Baal, "Master." We must bear in mind that Astarte's attendant in classical legend bears the name Adonis, that is to say Adon—the suffix *-is* is a purely Greek termination. In the Canaanite or Phoenician language Adon means "Lord," while Baal, as we have just noted, is "Master." These are two expressions of equal value, synonyms which can be interchanged, and which often were so transposed. Both are invocatory names; I shall have more to say about this matter later on.

Virolleaud has put the myth together from fragments. I shall not take it up in its entirety, but only draw upon as much of it as is pertinent at this point. We are told that one day Baal left the watchful Anat in order to hunt on the plains below the holy mountain, Safôn. He encountered a large number of wild creatures, which are named "the devouring," beings of human aspect crowned by horns. They overcame him and left his lifeless body on the plain, where the goddess, after long search, found it. With the help of the Sun Goddess, Anat took the body of her dead god, which she called "the world's beauty," up to Safôn and buried it. After this she sacrificed seventy animals on six successive occasions, so that the god might have nourishment in the underworld until his resurrection.

Experience taught that Baal's death occurred annually, and that unfailingly the god was reborn after six months. But, in spite of this, one was full of sorrow and anxiety, especially should the first rains be delayed or fail to come down in sufficient abundance. Every year the end of the world seemed imminent. When this did not occur, it was only because the goddess, seeking after Baal's brother and murderer, Môt—which means "Death,"—found him, and killed him with a scythe as the reaper cuts grain, and cast his remains to the winds. Baal could only return when the earth was again covered with new herbage—not only the symbol of life, but life itself, without which both men and gods could not live. Anat was not only an incarnate nature power, among many others; she was the power of nature in general, the soul of all things, as Virolleaud expresses it (*Eranos-Jahrbuch*, 1938, p. 157).

We know that *Dea Syria* of classical times was considered the mate of a Baal. But even here the female divinity was the more important and has been interpreted as a founding goddess of a city and state, who instituted both civil and religious life. It was she who taught mankind law and worship of the gods, and she is praised as the benefactress and protector who is to be thanked for all good. In the main, however, she is the goddess of all fertility, a universal deity, but particularly associated with water and fish. She is interpreted as the mother who feeds everything animate, and in this character is assimilated with Rhea and Cybele. In late cult legend she is brought into close association with the dove, which reputedly hatched her from an egg which the fish found in the water and brought to the shore—a legend of etiological character which arose by way of explanation of the reason why the Syrians did not eat fish and looked upon doves as holy.

The male partner who stands at her side is Adonis, who very early won a position in Greek cult by the side of Aphrodite. Adonis is the beautiful youth who dies and is wept over, after having been wedded to the great nature goddess as we meet her in Cyprus. Being immortal herself, she mourns annually over the loss of her lover, who dies when the vegetation wastes away.

The "Gardens of Adonis," so well known in classical literature, are closely tied to the Adonis cult. Seeds were sown in potsherds; these flowered quickly, but just as quickly withered away. It is certainly not without significance that they were sown in potsherds, as is pointed out by Dümmler in his article, "Adonis," in Pauly-Wissowa, *Real-Encyclopädie*, I, p. 388. He says: "Vielleicht war ursprünglich das Zerbrechen der Töpfe selbst ein Teil der Feier, eine Darstellung des Versiegens der Quellen, das den Tod des Adonis zur Folge hat." For my part, I am more inclined to see therein an implication that the seal of death has been broken and that life has reawakened. I would remind you of the widespread custom in ancient times throughout the Orient of burying the dead in storage vessels (cf. above, p. 13), and that in my view we have a Mycenaean "Garden of Adonis" depicted on our signet ring no. 24. That in later times seeds were sown in just such potsherds is a pregnant expression of the assurance of resurrection—that assurance which marks the entire cult of Adonis.

In the fifteenth Idyll of Theokritos the festival of Adonis in Alexandria is graphically described; first come the nuptials of Adonis and Aphrodite, represented by particolored statues, and then the sorrow and grief over the death of Adonis, which assume the most violent expression. We have a peculiar parallel in the very old Cretan custom which Plutarch describes in *De defectu oraculorum* XIV. In Crete a festival is celebrated during which an image of a headless man is shown, and it is said that such was Meriones' father, Molos, and that he was found thus after having assaulted a nymph. Molos is apparently a vegetation divinity, who, like Adonis, died immediately after the nuptials.

The Greek Adonis legends that have been preserved to our time are comparatively late but show striking similarity with the legends in the Ras Shamrah texts. The goddess Astarte met Adonis in the woods of Lebanon at the season when the anemones were in flower; that is, in the spring. Some months later, Adonis, while hunting, was killed by a wild animal. Astarte, alone and inconsolable, determined to go down to the underworld and snatch Adonis from Death. She succeeded in bringing the young god up into the light of day. After washing his wounds, she covered them with the choicest salves, and to her indescribable joy he was restored to life. In brief, this is the myth in its poetic form. Its touch on men's hearts was so lasting that devotees of Adonis were known even into the fourth century A.D.

We can conclude from the collective evidence of the sources that from olden times the Adonis cult was a native one in Phoenicia, especially in Byblos and on Lebanon. Lucian says (*De dea Syria*, 6 f.) that Adonis was mortally wounded by a wild boar and that the river which flows by Hierapolis was colored red throughout the days prior to his death. At that time the festival of Adonis was celebrated with great signs of sorrow. The women offered their hair or gave their bodies for a price and brought their earnings as a gift to the goddess. After they have wept and grieved, they first bring a sacrifice to Adonis as to one dead; but on the following day he is declared to be alive again. Death and resurrection are thus the characteristics of Adonis. Consequently, he is to be associated most intimately with the Babylonian Tammuz, with whom he is often identified, as well as with the Egyptian Osiris and the Phrygian Attis. With both of these, Adonis has both factual and historical associations, as Frazer has pointed out.

The accounts differ radically concerning the time of year when the festival of Adonis was held; it is more than likely that in the course of historical time various episodes of the divine drama were incorporated, in midsummer, into a great festival, although originally these individual acts of the drama belonged to those seasons of the year which they depicted.

At this point we must not overlook entirely the Babylonian goddess, Ishtar, from time immemorial associated with the evening star, the planet Venus, but also simultaneously a goddess representing life itself. The myth which is associated with her is known to us only in a fragmentary form, primarily through the Gilgamesh epic, the great Babylonian heroic poem about the King of Uruk. It is told of Gilgamesh that, after doing battle with the giants on the Cedar Mount, he returned victorious to his city. He polished his weapons, put on new attire, allowed his loose hair to fall down over his shoulders, and wound a fresh wreath about his forehead. All the women of the land looked up with wonder at the victorious king, and even the goddess, Ishtar, raised her eyes up to him and said: "Come, Gilgamesh, and be my husband." She promised him a carriage of lapis lazuli and gold, and mighty horses, and that all princes and kings should do obeisance before him and bring him offerings. Gilgamesh harshly disdained her proposals and chid her for her inconstancy. For it was known that she had cast off all who loved her, and changed them into animals which she ruthlessly hunted—all except Tammuz, her first love, who died young. In tribute to his memory, mankind and all nature were made to commemorate his death yearly. Nevertheless, the goddess turned her love to others, only to cast them off after a short time, when she would transform them, one to a bird the wings of which she broke; one to a lion; one to a horse; and one, a shepherd, she changed into a leopard so that his own hounds pursued him and tore him asunder—as the hunter Aktaion was changed by Artemis into a deer and torn apart by his own dogs in the Greek saga. In the Babylonian epic Ishtar is a kind of Circe, and Gilgamesh did not want to share the fate which befell Odysseus' companions in later times.

The old Mesopotamian sagas contribute the short account of Ishtar's journey to the underworld. One day she decided to go down to that land from which no one had ever returned, where the souls of the dead were exposed to misery and darkness, nourished only by eating of the very earth in which they lay. She ordered the guardian of the shadowy kingdom to open the door, and after much dispute she came into her sister's realm. She wished to fetch the dead to the world of light in order to destroy the living, the epic says. Her sister was very much displeased by the visit, yet permitted her to enter, on condition that every time she passed through a portal—there were seven of them—she would strip herself of some part of her ornaments or dress. Thus Ishtar lost her crown, her necklace, her girdle, and finally the robe that covered her. When she came into the innermost room she was naked and powerless, and, bearing no longer the signs of her power, she became a prisoner among the dead.

While she was detained there, all life ceased on the face of the earth. Seeds did not ripen, plants died, all living beings, men and beasts, did not procreate. The world was threatened by dissolution. The gods themselves suffered for want of food and offerings of thanks. This, of course, reminds us unavoidably of Demeter's sorrow in the Homeric Hymn to Demeter. Finally, the god of wisdom is forced to intervene and orders that Ishtar return by the very way she entered and in so doing recover her habiliments. As soon as the goddess returns to earth again, all life begins anew. In the last verses mention is made of Tammuz; and it is credible that the whole account of her visit depends upon a plan to bring his soul from the underworld—a parallel to the Adonis myth,—but definitive evidence is lacking. In another hymn Tammuz is compared to a tender plant growing on poorly watered ground and bringing forth no flowers; we recall the "Garden of Adonis." Yet Tammuz never assumes so significant a place with Ishtar as Adonis does in relation to Astarte, or Osiris to Isis. Tammuz was Ishtar's first love, whereas the other two are the only loves of Astarte and Isis.

The Isis and Osiris myth does not demand more than brief treatment here. Isis is indisputably the most popular of all Egyptian divinities, and her worshipers were to be found far beyond her native borders. Her cult was widespread because she was so often identified with foreign divinities. Within Greek lands, she was thought of along with Selene and Io, primarily because she wore a cow's head in Egypt, while her association with Demeter derived from her native role of creator of harvests. The spike and the horn of plenty are her symbols; the cow, representing the earth and agriculture, is her sacred animal. She is compared to Aphrodite, and her son, Horus, to Eros. She protects women while they suckle their young and is also a sort of divinity of medicine as well as a goddess of sorcery. Even as a sea goddess she is entitled to worship, and in Greek lands she is called Pelagia. At the side of this great, almost universal goddess, we meet her brother and husband, Osiris, who plays a subordinate role. This relationship leads to that peculiar consequence whereby the goddess is regarded as chief protectress to her fraternal spouse. The Osiris myth is the most cherished of all Egyptian sagas; we know it best through a late account by Plutarch, *De Iside et Osiride*. The Egyptian narratives often show contradictory features, but in general verify the account given by Plutarch while at the same time they supplement it. Here is the Osiris myth in brief.

Osiris, son to the god of Heaven, had succeeded to the sovereignty of earth and reigned for many years over men and gods as a just, wise, and brave king. His brother, Typhon, or Seth, who symbolized all waste places as well as uncouthness and utter barbarism, envied his power and conspired against his life. Isis, the wise wife of Osiris, tried in every way through her powers of sorcery to protect her husband, but finally, by guile, Seth managed to take Osiris' life. According to one tradition, his body, enclosed in a chest, was cast into the sea, and finally after a long search was found by Isis in Byblos, where it had drifted to shore and become entangled in a tamarisk, which had grown about it; the king had made himself a column for his palace from the tree, and it was then that Isis learned of the fate of Osiris and came to Byblos. She met the women attendants of the king, told them of her bad fortune, and won them over by promising to give them precious ointments and to teach them to dress their hair after the Egyptian fashion. Thus she entered the palace and narrated her ill fortune to the king and asked him for the body of her dead mate. Greatly moved by compassion, the king gave her the column in which the body of Osiris was enclosed.

According to the interpretation generally accepted at the present time, the column is reproduced in the Egyptian fetish which is named Zed or Ded. This is a columnar shaft with four protruding parts lying on top of one another, interpreted earlier by Champollion as a nilometer, by others as an altar with four superimposed slabs or a series of four columns.

As the legend continues, Seth learned that Isis had found the body of Osiris, and he managed to get possession of it, cut it into bits, and scattered its parts over the whole land. Sorrowfully Isis searched after the dismembered parts of her beloved husband, and when she had finally found them all, she and her sister Nephtys lamented over them. Anubis, the god with the jackal head, embalmed the body of Osiris, and Isis, through her powers of sorcery, was able to awaken life in the corpse. But Osiris was incapable of dwelling longer on earth and therefore retired to the underworld, where he became king and ruler of the realm of the dead.

As Frazer has pointed out (cf. *The Golden Bough*, IV, 2, p. 201), there is to be found in the three Oriental divinities Attis, Adonis, and Osiris an embodiment of the powers of fertility in general and of vegetation in particular; and of agriculture, especially important for man, I should add. All three are believed to have died and to have risen from the dead. The death and resurrection of the deities was depicted dramatically at the annual festivals, which worshipers celebrated with ecstatic expressions of sorrow and joy. The phenomena of nature, thus interpreted and represented mystically, were the great seasonal changes—above all, the death and renewal of vegetation. The purpose of the cult practices was to strengthen the declining strength of nature through sympathetic magic in order that the trees should bear fruit, the seeds ripen, and men and animals perpetuate their kind. But none of these three deities stood alone.

The great nature goddess, however, the Goddess Mother, has an area of influence and of expansion much larger than that which has been touched on here; everywhere she has the same character. She is the goddess of the earth, but also of the water, since both of these elements are requisite for the existence of vegetation; she also becomes the goddess of heaven and of light. Altogether, she is the goddess of life, the incarnation of eternal life. She alone is to be worshiped, that life may be perpetuated from generation to generation, that procreation may always be continued. The young male god embodies, not perpetual life, but transitory life—that which rises anew every spring, matures in the summer season, and withers away in the autumn. He is the life of vegetation on which the existence of men and animals and gods depends, for gods can exist only if man provides food for them, the meat of animals and the blood of the vine.

When mankind reaches a stage of development at which an implemented agriculture begins to appear in the great river valleys, this god becomes of greater significance as an agricultural deity. With the help of divine power, man has acquired the ability to bring forth from the earth produce, which, however, he does not permit to run its natural course; he harvests before the plant withers away. To the seed which has suddenly become so essential for man a special guardian is given, sometimes the son of the great goddess of nature and earth, sometimes her youthful husband or lover. He dies young, only to rise again. The grain is harvested, and corn of the harvest, after the fallow months, is again strewn to bring forth a new harvest.

In an article entitled "La Flagellation rituelle," in *Cultes, Mythes et Religions*, I, pp. 173 ff., Salomon Reinach has shown that ritualistic scourging appears everywhere in the cult of the Great Mother, she who watches over the renewal of life, and he has maintained that this scourging should be considered as a means of waking the powers of the earth at the time of renascence, exactly as one harrows Mother Earth before the seed is sown.

Apparently in all the religions which we have observed, the Great Goddess has originally been a mightier and more important figure than the god. It is the god, not the goddess, who dies and is yearly mourned. We can best understand the superiority of the Goddess if, as suggested above, we regard the god as a representative of vegetation and agriculture. An auxiliary factor is to be taken into account, namely, the primitive social system, in which the dominant fact was matriarchy, birth and right of inheritance following the maternal line and not that of the father. Frazer has treated such matriarchies as they occur in primitive society.

After this survey of the beliefs obtaining in the lands near Crete, beliefs which can be traced back to the time with which we are specifically concerned, namely, the second millennium B.C., we return to Crete itself. As I have already taken occasion to observe, it is quite certain that even in Crete the two central deities are a great Mother Goddess and, by her side, a youth, a kind of consort. Naturally, I do not go so far as to identify those deities with their counterparts in the Near East and in Egypt; we must not overlook the fact that the causes and circumstances of religious conceptions depend on various basic factors operative in any one region, above all on changes and differences due to climatic and geographic conditions. The root of the matter is this—that we are justified in seeing our Minoan-Mycenaean divinities under precisely these aspects.

Judging by all the evidences, the great Mother Goddess in Crete had been from the beginning a universal deity, the goddess of nature herself, like the Great Goddess in Asia Minor, Syria, and Egypt. She has been a figure originally with vague contours, with different qualities, manifestations, and attributes, a nebula, of which in time certain parts, gradually detached, have received new and clearer contours from reflection and increasing personification. Consequently, in view of the Oriental parallels, I share

Evans' first basic interpretation of the Great Goddess in Crete, and must confess that I find it difficult to attach any decisive significance to the general arguments with which Nilsson (*Minoan-Mycenaean Religion*, pp. 337 f.) has opposed it in his discussion of unity and variety. Marinatos has recently expressed a decided opinion in favor of *one* goddess (cf. *Ephemeris Archaiologike*, 1937, p. 290).

In accordance with the parallels from the religions discussed, we may rightfully consider the youthful male god, the consort of the Great Goddess, as a representative of the yearly vegetation, especially in its connection with agriculture.

Out of these two deities, the Great Goddess and the Boy God, there later developed a larger number of more or less distinct figures, which we meet with in Greek religious myths. In my opinion, their multiple variety depends to a very considerable degree on the different invocatory names, the *epikleseis*, of originally one and the same deity. It will be our task to consider this feature, as well as other traces of Minoan-Mycenaean religion in the Greek religion, in the following chapter.

CHAPTER FIVE

MINOAN-MYCENAEAN SURVIVALS IN THE GREEK RELIGION OF CLASSICAL TIMES

ARIADNE, about whom a rich web of tradition was spun, is one of the most interesting figures in Greek mythology. In his biography of Theseus, Plutarch has given us some valuable examples of her myths.

Ariadne had apparently been an important goddess with a widespread cult. The various sagas of the different cult places gained high respect and popularity until the classical period, when they became mutually contradictory. In his *Griechische Feste*, pp. 382 ff., Nilsson has tried to explain the changing myths as a consequence of cult conflicts. The great goddess, Ariadne, had come into conflict with overpowering rivals, in part with Aphrodite, in part with Dionysos, particularly on the islands of the Aegean Sea. As a result of this antagonism the cult of Ariadne disappeared. This dissolution was accounted for in the Homeric hymns by the avowal that Dionysos had caused the death of Ariadne. On the other hand, the cults of Ariadne and Dionysos were to some degree connected with one another, and this found expression in the myth in which Dionysos took Ariadne to wife.

It is of great interest to look closely at the name Ariadne. It occurs in different forms. By the side of Ariadne the form Ariagne also appears in the inscriptions, both for the goddess and later as a personal name (cf. *C. I. G.*, 7441, 7691, *I. G. I.*, 758 f.). For an explanation of this form it is sufficient to refer to the gloss by Hesychios ἀδνόν · ἁγνόν . Κρῆτες; thus Ariadne means "the very holy." 'Αρι-, according to Boisacq, *Dictionnaire étymologique de la langue grecque*, is: "Particule inséparable exprimant l'idée d'aptitude, de supériorité"; cf. ἀρίγνωτος, ἀρίδακρυς, ἀρίδηλος—"much"; cf.

also Brugmann in *Indogermanische Forschungen*, 1895, pp. 379 f.

Hesychios offers also another gloss, Ἀριδήλαν·τὴν Ἀριάδνην. Κρῆτες. In the second part of the name the adjective δῆλος, "visible," is hidden. Thus the name means "the very visible" and has nearly the same significance as Pasiphae, "the one visible to all."

As I see it, we are dealing with obvious invocations in both of these names. Both are primarily adjectival, raised secondarily to proper names, to be understood as invocatory forms of the deity: "Thou very sacred One"; "Thou very visible One."

That invocation, ἐπίκλησις, played a significant role during the second millennium B.C. seems to me most evident from the fact that in Egyptian royal inscriptions, for example, we find the use of extensive invocation and pyramiding of titles addressed to the kings, and to their public officials also; compare, for example, in Erman-Ranke's *Aegypten*, pp. 59 f., the titles in the dating of a monumental stone which was erected in the time of Rameses II on the road to the Nubian gold mines. It is to be presumed that the gods, too, were thus originally invoked by a multitude of adjectival attributes which later were elevated into proper names.

We possess even from classical times a type of hymn called ὕμνος κλητικός, the "calling of the God." One such hymn bearing these ancient implications is the Cretan Hymn of the Kouretes, which begins

Ἰώ, μέγιστε Κοῦρε,
χαῖρέ μοι, Κρόνειε,
παγκρατὲς γάνος, βέβακες . . .

that is, "Io, Kouros most great, I give thee hail, Kronian, Almighty Gleam, thou art come . . ." (cf. Harrison, *Themis*, pp. 7 ff.).

In the *Carmen Saeculare* of Horace we have a late copy of such a ὕμνος κλητικός. The poet invokes, as is known, Apollo and Diana.

> Phoebe silvarumque potens Diana,
> lucidum caeli decus, o colendi
> semper et culti, date ...

In verse 9 he turns to Apollo with "alme Sol"; in verses 14 ff., again to Diana:

> ... Ilithyia, tuere matres,
> sive tu Lucina probas vocari
> seu Genitalis.

In verse 34, again to Apollo and then to Diana:

> ... supplices audi pueros, Apollo;
> siderum regina bicornis, audi,
> Luna, puellas.

It is apparent that Horace follows on this occasion a well-known Greek pattern. We see the role which the adjectival determinants occupy, and how they have sometimes become solidified into epithets or by-names. It is clear that Lucina (< *lux*) is comparable to Pasiphae, and we should not miss the fact that the goddess is invoked as *Luna, siderum regina bicornis*. The importance of invocatory names appears also clearly and plainly from the words of the poet: *sive tu Lucina probas vocari seu Genitalis*.

We may well suppose that the Achaeans in Crete heard the deities invoked in this manner; we meet with native Cretan invocations, and translations into the Achaean language of such invocations also occur. With their strong natural inclination for making concrete and personifying all abstraction, these invocations were translated by the Greeks into the personified shapes of the gods. These shapes each reflect one aspect of the basic divinity, and these still later were spun out into the rich mythology we know. In my view, then, the cult itself was instrumental in the shaping of myths in the same way that historical events are instrumental in the shaping of legends.

A like name is Britomartis, or Britamartis, as she is called in the Delian inscriptions,[1] but with the difference that this name has a non-Grecian, that is, Cretan connotation. A gloss in Hesychios says, Βριτύ·γλυκύ; Κρῆτες; *Etymologicum Magnum*, p. 214, line 29, has: Βρίτον, τουτέστιν ἀγαθόν; and Solinus XI, 8, says: "Britomartem, quod sermone nostro sonat virginem dulcem." What we have here is undoubtedly a remnant of the Minoan language, and thus we get in Hesychios' gloss Βριτόμαρτις·ἐν Κρήτῃ ἡ Ἄρτεμις an explanation of the original nature of the goddess. Diodoros, V, 76, 3, has the same identification.

Now the myth relates that Britomartis was one of Artemis' hunting comrades and that she was especially loved by her, which may show that her character was the same as that of Artemis. All this lends support to the supposition that she was an ancient goddess in Crete; moreover, she was a deity whose name was commonly used in oaths in Knossos, Dreros, and in a compact between Lato and Olus. In the last-mentioned city her festival was celebrated in classical times, and there also was a very old statue, a *xoanon* of her, made by Daidalos. She had a temple in Cherronesos, the port town of Lythos. Consequently we can assert that she was a deity specially bound to Crete, where her cult was spread on the north coast from Knossos to the cove of Mirabello. In classical times the name of the goddess was preserved as an epithet and by-name for Artemis. The name Britomartis originates from the invocation: "Thou sweet virgin."

I regard Diktynna, closely associated with Britomartis, as another such name. A myth related by Kallimachos tells us that Britomartis at one time was pursued by Minos,

---

[1] Cf. Nilsson, *Minoan-Mycenaean Religion*, pp. 438 ff., for Britomartis, Diktynna, and Aphaia.

who had fallen in love with her. In order to escape him she threw herself into the sea, but she was saved by falling into the net of some fishermen. Thereafter she was known as Diktynna, δίκτυον being the Greek word for net. In *Minoan-Mycenaean Religion*, p. 440, Nilsson has rightly established that she was a Cretan goddess, much like Artemis, a double for Britomartis, who was worshiped in eastern, whereas Diktynna had her cult places chiefly in western Crete.

The etymology for the name Diktynna as adduced by Kallimachos may appear satisfactory. On the other hand, it seems obvious that the name was originally connected with the well-known mountain in Crete, Dikte. This mountain, however, lies inland in the eastern part of the island, while the cult of Diktynna, as we have mentioned, is met with primarily in its western part. Yet Mingazzini, in his article "Culti e miti preellenici in Creta" (*Religio*, 1919, pp. 276 f.), has indicated a way out of the dilemma. He suggests that the chaotic events in Crete may have forced her cult out of its original home to a more active worship in comparatively foreign areas. Parallels to this are not hard to find; and likewise when a cult is moved from one localized home to another, the deity is given an appellation which recalls the original home. Thus we get Apollo Pythios and Delios, or Zeus Labrandeus, the god from Labranda. It may be quite likely that the Great Goddess was worshiped on the mountain Dikte under the invocatory name Britomartis, while in the western part of Crete she was invoked as "Thou who dwellest on Dikte."

We hear also of a deity who went under the name of Aphaia. Late writers (Antoninus Liberalis, 40, and Pausanias, II, 30, 3) relate that Britomartis came to Aegina and there disappeared into a grove, where a temple was later built to her. There may be an etymological connection between the name Aphaia and the word ἀφανής, "unseen, invisible." Wilamowitz thinks that the original name of the goddess was Apha—it is found in this form in an inscription, *I. G.*, IV, 1582. Aphaia would then be an adjective derived from Apha, analogous to Athenaia, from Athene. (*Sitzungsberichte der Berliner Akademie*, 1921, p. 952, n. 1.) I am not entirely convinced that the adjective form is later than the noun. I think that her name in the beginning was an invocatory adjective of the Ariadne type. Aphaia is seldom mentioned in classical literature; it is only Hesychios who left us the note, Ἀφαία·ἡ Δικτύννα, καὶ Ἄρτεμις; but she has become famous in our day as a result of the impressive temple in Aegina, which inscriptions prove to have been dedicated to her.

All the deities who have been mentioned and who have characteristics in common with Artemis are but illuminations of special facets of the Great Goddess in Crete. Nilsson has, I believe, successfully demonstrated the derivation of the classical goddesses from their prototype the Cretan Great Goddess.

A common nickname for Artemis in her character of Goddess of Childbearing is Eileithyia. From Nilsson's discussion of this deity it seems certain that Eileithyia is of pre-Grecian origin (cf. *Minoan-Mycenaean Religion*, pp. 446 ff.). She was worshiped especially in Crete, on the near-by islands, and in Lakonia. This makes it probable that she is of Minoan origin. Von der Loeff and Malten have joined together the names Eileithyia and Eleusis, and to these Malten has also added Elysion. With respect to the etymology of the word group in question, Schulze (*Quaestiones Epicae*, pp. 260 ff.) wishes to associate them with the Greek word stem, ἐλευθ-, to "come," but Wackernagel prefers to see in the stem a pre-Grecian element, without, however, entirely denying Schulze's suggestion. In any event, Eileithyia is obviously a name which should be coupled with the Great Goddess in Crete. After the pattern suggested, I see it as an invocatory name, either of

Greek origin, "Thou who comest," of the Ariadne type; or of Minoan origin, of the Britomartis type.

It may be fitting at this point to consider one or two other Cretan mythical figures.[2] Let us examine that of Pasiphae first. Pasiphae, the wife of Minos, conceived an unnatural love for a bull. She satisfied her desire by hiding within the effigy of a cow—in classical times Daidalos was credited with the making of the effigy,—and Minotaur was the result of that union. As Picard has suggested (*Revue de Philologie*, 1933, pp. 344 ff.), it seems very probable that the basic feature of the legend is of Egyptian origin, and that in some bizarre way it underwent a change by its exegesis. Picard properly points out that in Herodotos, II, 129 f., it is related that the Pharaoh Mykerinos, when his daughter died, had her buried within a gilded wooden cow, the customary Hathor symbol. Mykerinos placed the cow in his palace in Sais, where the image was still worshiped in the time of Herodotos; it was constantly surrounded by burning lamps and clouds of incense. It is Picard's contention that the Minoans had adopted and then transmitted to the Mycenaeans the cult of the sacred kine—of either sex—in all its forms, with its adjunct of preservative powers, which supposedly extended even into the life after this.

In the Pasiphae myth the bull is anonymous; Pasiphae, on the other hand, is a transparently significant name, that of the "all-illuminating," the "visible to all." In mythographical literature she appears as the daughter of the sun; she herself was a moon goddess, according to the various comments of classical writers. I shall only refer to Pausanias, III, 26, 1, who says that there was at Thalamai a sanctuary with images of Helios and Pasiphae. Pasiphae, he adds, is "an invocatory name for Selene—Σελήνης δὲ

[2] Cf. my contribution, "Legende und Mythos in ihrem Verhältnis zu Bild und Gleichnis im vorgeschichtlichen Griechenland," in ΔΡΑΓΜΑ *Martino P. Nilsson dedicatum*, pp. 379 ff., esp. pp. 396 ff.

ἐπίκλησις—and not a local deity among the inhabitants of Thalamai."

The corresponding adjective πασιφαής is to be met with quite often, not only in connection with the sun, but also with the moon (cf. Roscher, *Ueber Selene und Verwandtes*, p. 7). The old legendary content in the Pasiphae myth is clear to us if we associate the cow-figured goddess with the classical moon goddess, Selene, who was often conceived of as a cow—she was commonly represented in anthropomorphic fashion with horns; cow or bull horns were regarded very early in Egypt as symbols for the crescent moon. The bull in the legend is the God of Heaven and Fertility whom we have already met in the Near East and in Crete. This has been dealt with by Malten in his article, "Der Stier in Kult und mythischem Bild," *Archäologisches Jahrbuch*, 1928, pp. 90 ff.

We come next to Europa and the Bull. According to the saga, Europa was the beautiful daughter of the Phoenician king Agenor. Zeus fell in love with her when he happened to see her with her playmates, picking flowers on the shore. He approached her in the guise of a bull. Europa petted the handsome beast. Finally, she climbed upon its back, whereupon the bull plunged into the sea and carried her off to Crete; and there she became the mother of Minos.

The bull, in this myth called Zeus, is our old acquaintance from the Orient and from Crete, the Bull of Heaven and Fertility. During classical times he was known in Crete by the name of Zeus Asterios, that is, Zeus of the Stars. Europa shows a number of parallels to the Moon Goddess which we need not dwell upon here; we must content ourselves merely with a reference to Roscher's *Selene und Verwandtes*. But there is one matter which requires comment: Europa is often represented with a crescent-shaped veil over her head—which either in the same or in a somewhat more rounded form is otherwise characteristic of Selene's headgear—apparently symbolizing the clouds behind which the moon intermittently withdraws itself. On coins minted in Sidon, 111 B.C. to 117 A.D., we meet with the Sidonian Astarte, Σιδῶνος θεά according to the inscription, riding on a bull—precisely the same representation as that of Europa to be seen on coins from Gortyn in Crete.³

Of extraordinary interest is the fact that these late representations agree in every detail with the representations

Fig. 24. Glass plaque from Dendra-Midea, showing "Europa" on the bull, and an Egyptian design on papyrus showing the Moon God on the cow.

on some glass plaques from the King's Tomb at Dendra, excavated by the Swedish expedition in 1926. The tomb can be dated *circa* 1350 B.C. In these latter representations (cf. fig. 24) I venture to find Europa or her counterpart on the bull. The force of the comparison is somewhat weakened by the length of the time interval between the two groups of material, but it is impossible to deny the general agreement. Astarte and Europa on classical coins also have their equivalents during the second millennium B.C. Astarte is, to be sure, par excellence the naked goddess, and as the naked goddess she appears with exactly the same crescent veil much earlier on a group of Syro-Hittite seal cylinders

³ Technau deals more fully with the goddess on the bull in an interesting paper entitled "Die Göttin auf dem Stier," *Archäologisches Jahrbuch*, 1937, pp. 76 ff. I can, however, not agree with him in all points of view.

(cf. Contenau, *Manuel d'archéologie orientale*, p. 949). On these cylinders (cf. fig. 25) we actually find all our elements: the bull, the woman, and the veil, and furthermore, by the presence of moon and stars, an unmistakable indication of the celestial character of these representations. That Europa is not seen naked on the Dendra representation is due to the prudishness of Cretan art. Moreover, in the Oriental representations the goddess assumes another pos-

Fig. 25. Oriental cylinder seals showing the naked goddess above the bull.

ture with relation to the beast, that which is common for Hittite deities when riding on animals, and which is met with even in classical times in connection with Zeus Dolichenus.

Viewed for its effect as a composition, the Dendra representation resembles most closely the Egyptian images (cf. fig. 27), which show us the Sun God on his heavenly cow—note the hold on the one horn and the twist given to the animal's head. Note also the crossing of sexes, here a god on a cow, there a goddess on a bull. This undoubtedly accords with the different genders of the cosmic phenomena: in Egypt, the moon is a male god, Thot, the firmament is pictured as a star-bedecked woman; in Greece, the moon is a goddess, Selene, and the sky is Uranos. It therefore seems justifiable to regard Europa as a moon heroine. Her Oriental origin is evident from the statement in the myth that she was the daughter of a king of Phoenicia. But what does her name mean?

Since we know so much about Europa, I do not think it needful, along with Fick and Autrant, to create the difficulty of a foreign derivation. The suffix *-opa* is, of course, a well-known one, almost "glancing." But *eur-* presents a difficulty. After Roscher, one would prefer to combine it with εὐρύς, "widespread"—we have a Homeric epithet for Zeus, εὐρύοπα, apparently "wide-glancing." Roscher proceeds from εὐρ- in the word εὖρος, "width," but this seems to entail difficulties. Gruppe proposes a derivation which is morphologically easier, but which factually is not so convincing,—from εὐρω-, which is to be found in εὐρώεις and in the adjective εὐρωπός. Εὐρώεις is used especially of dark holes, and εὐρωπός should mean almost "dark," "dark-glancing," and, with normal accent changes in the building of the name, *Europa* could thus come to mean "the dark-glancing." If an invocation is in question here, then a vocative form may lie at the basis of the name. The accent changes do not cause us any difficulty.

Howsoever this be, the meaning should be sought in the way here indicated. In this fashion we get a parallel to Pasiphae, "the all-brightening." Both names are adjectival, and invocatory, "Thou all-illuminating," "Thou wide-glancing," or "dark-glancing." The conclusive point is that exactly the same cult background is seen to be behind both myths: Pasiphae and Europa are invocations of the same deity.

I hold that we are thus to regard ἐπίκλησις as the cause behind such nomenclature as that of Ariadne, "the very holy one," Aridela, "the very visible one," Britomartis, "the sweet virgin," Europa, "the wide- or dark-glancing one,"

Pasiphae, "the one visible to all," Diktynna, "she who is worshiped on Dikte," Eileithyia, perhaps "she who comes," and I do not hesitate to include Helen, "the shining one" (cf. Boisacq, *Dictionnaire étymologique*, s. v. ἑλάνη = torch, σέλας = light, Selene).

From the invocatory nomenclature of later deities we can thus trace some of the aspects of the earlier divinity: we can see that the original Great Goddess was also the goddess of the moon, according to the various phases of which she later on came to be known as Pasiphae, Europa, Aridela, Aphaia, or Helen. In Oriental religions we find that the Great Goddess played a similar role—she was moon goddess as well as the universal goddess of fertility. Moreover, this double function actually corresponds to a close association between certain phenomena in nature, since the moon is a necessary adjunct to vegetational fertility by virtue of its quickening dews in the comparatively rainless lands of the South.

We even find that the male deity, the original Boy God, is later named after a similar fashion. We have already mentioned Glaukos as "the gray-blue one." Hyakinthos, the name of a prehistoric deity absorbed by Apollo—note the -*nt*- stem—was also the hyacinth plant (or, more correctly, the iris or gladiolus) and the color of this plant. The Hyakinthos festival, the *Hyakinthia*, was one of the largest and most sacred festivals in Lakonia, celebrated yearly in Amyklai near Sparta in the month of Hekatombeus, which probably was equivalent to the Athenian *Thargelion*. The later saga relates that Hyakinthos was the youthful lover of Apollo, who accidentally killed him by a careless throw of the discus. Hyakinthos lay buried under an altar-like edifice, on which was placed the ancient bronze image of Apollo; a low bronze door beside the altar enabled the worshiper to send down parts of the sacrificial animals to the dead during the festival. We have a description of the festival itself in Athenaios (IV, 139 d ff.). All Sparta participated in the commemoration of the hero Hyakinthos, and the festival lasted at least three days. Great strictness was observed during the sacrificial meal on the first day; only certain dishes were allowed, and music and wreaths and paeans were forbidden. The first day was a solemn festival. But on the day following, joy and gaiety reigned, as was customary at festivals. Wreaths were worn, paeans were sung, and everyone, even stranger and slave, was richly entertained. Boys handsomely dressed performed dances, and female choirs sang and later took part in an evening entertainment.

The relationship of Hyakinthos to Adonis, Attis, and Osiris, other representatives of the yearly vegetation, is transparent. The important *-nt-* element of the name vouches for the pre-Grecian Minoan origin of the god. It would seem that Apollo had usurped the festival of Hyakinthos, and that the older god had been degraded to the position of a hero. Apollo even usurped the name, since he came to be called Apollo Hyakinthos. The same Hyakinthos is to be found on Knidos, where we hear of Artemis Hyakinthotrophos, who had a temple and a festival. Her name means "the nurse of Hyakinthos."

Nilsson has pointed out the similarity between Hyakinthos and the Cretan Zeus (cf. *Minoan-Mycenaean Religion*, p. 486). The latter was also reputed to have been a child who was not reared by his mother; but the nurse of Hyakinthos is neither animal nor nymph, but the mistress of all beasts, the pre-Grecian goddess Artemis. Nilsson states, and rightly, that we are justified in assuming that the Cretan Zeus and Hyakinthos, both of whom are pre-Grecian, represent one and the same god of vegetation under different names. That Hyakinthos also names a flower is but confirmatory evidence for his connection with the vegetation cult.

The name of Erichthonios is apparently derived from χθών, "earth," and the prefix ἐρι-, "much." One myth relates that Athena, who received the little Erichthonios from *Ge*, "the Earth,"—Herodotus, VIII, 55, says specifically that he was born of the earth,—laid the child in a chest together with snakes and had the three nymphs Aglauros, Pandrosos, and Herse take care of it. Observe that here also a child is not nursed by its mother the grain-bearing earth; and Erichthonios is apparently, as Nilsson maintains (*Minoan-Mycenaean Religion*, p. 490), a divine child like Plutos at Eleusis, the newborn vegetation spirit, who was handed over to others to be nurtured. The nymphs set over the child all have obvious names—Aglauros, "the bright one," Pandrosos, "the all-dewy one," and Herse, again "the dew"; that is to say, they represent the atmospheric elements which hasten the growth of vegetation. In representational art, Erichthonios is pictured as half human and half snake, his body tapering to a serpent's tail. This circumstance is a reminder of the prominent place which the snake occupies in the Eleusinian cult, where it is especially associated with the agricultural hero Triptolemos, and again of the snake of Zeus Ktesios, who guards the storeroom and the stored grain; compare also the snake in the Glaukos myth. Nilsson has also drawn attention to the fact that Erichthonios is bound firmly to the oldest cults on the Acropolis. He shared a temple with Athena, who was herself of Minoan-Mycenaean origin. The position of the Erechtheion in our day speaks eloquently for the fact that this old sanctuary was situated within the Mycenaean palace on the Acropolis. And that Erichthonios goes back to Mycenaean times is quite certain.

Another subordinate deity whose name is easily understood is Eubouleus, "good in advice." Eubouleus had a place in the Eleusinian Mysteries, and cannot be separated from Zeus Bouleus, who receives sacrifices along with Demeter and Kore on Mykonos and neighboring islands. It is an interesting survival to see Zeus here in a circle of agricultural divinities.

In *Minoan-Mycenaean Religion*, Nilsson has given much space to an attempt to show the survival of the Minoan-Mycenaean religion in Greek religion proper (pp. 385–560). Given the new points of departure, we must revise the entire history of Greek religion, which at this point, however, would demand too much of our time.[4] I only wish to supplement Nilsson's discussion on some points. We must, undoubtedly, agree with Nilsson that we have "a very strong cumulative evidence for the continuity of Mycenaean cults in the Greek age" (p. 414). We must allow for Greek deities of Minoan-Mycenaean origin in the castle at Mycenae, on the Acropolis in Athens, and quite certainly in Tiryns also. At one time the prince had been a priest-king and his religious functions were considerable, so that the name king was preserved, even in later times, for the one who retained his religious functions after his political importance had disappeared.

Nilsson has collected weighty evidence to prove that Minoan-Mycenaean elements are to be found not only in Greek cults, but also, and very tangibly, in many of the Greek deities. But first a few words about the most immediate predecessors to these gods, Rhea and Kronos, as we find them interpreted in Greek mythology.

Concerning the pre-Grecian origin of Rhea, it is my opinion that we are justified in stating this fact with greater certainty than Nilsson permits himself (cf. *Minoan-Mycenaean Religion*, pp. 464 f.). Nilsson admits that she is to be compared in her character of Mother Goddess with Cybele, as has been done by earlier writers. But the difference he stresses so emphatically, that Rhea had a spouse in Kronos

[4] Cf. the forthcoming treatment by Nilsson in Müllers *Handbuch der klassischen Altertumswissenschaft*. Through the kindness of the author I had the opportunity to see the proofs of the first part of this important work.

and that she is the mother of his children, especially Zeus, should not confuse us when we observe that the related events in Egypt are of the same kind. There we have Isis and Osiris and their son Horus. Even in Greek mythology Rhea is the more prominent of the divine pair. Considering the general similarity, Kronos can very well be an agricultural or vegetational god, or, as Nilsson says, a god of the harvest, a designation which can just as easily be applied to Attis, Adonis, and Osiris. To my mind, the parallel is more than apt, and it is my opinion that it is more than plausible that even Kronos is an old pre-Grecian god.

The myth, known from Homer and exhaustively treated in Hesiod's *Theogonia*, relates that Rhea gave birth to Zeus as the youngest in a series of divine children. When Kronos wished to devour him as he had devoured the others, Rhea hid the child and gave Kronos a stone instead, wrapped in swaddling clothes, which he swallowed. We have here a reminder of the aniconic image of the deity, the stone, in Minoan-Mycenaean religion. Kronos was able to disgorge the stone as well as the brothers and sisters of Zeus, and, according to the legend, the stone was placed in Delphi—a new proof connecting the omphalos with the worship of the stone in Cretan-Mycenaean religion.

The cult places of Rhea seem to me also very significant. According to Diodoros, V, 66, 1, there was to be found near Knossos a temple of Rhea where on her orders the Kouretes performed their armed dance. Pernier (cf. *Saggi di storia antica e di archeologia offerti a Gi. Beloch*, 1910, pp. 241 f.) has authenticated a Rhea temple at Phaistos. According to Pausanias, I, 18, 7, she had a temple in Athens along with Kronos, and, VIII, 36, 2, in Arcadia a cave sanctuary, high up in the mountains. Her altar in Olympia is of course of later date, but is nevertheless a witness of the great age of this figure; and the myth about the birth of Zeus was undoubtedly the occasion for this cult. Rhea received sacrifices on Kos, and she even had a cult in Miletos (cf. Nilsson, *Griechische Feste*, p. 444).

Her name is enigmatic, but all efforts to explain its etymology point in the same direction. Most presumable seems to me a sound displacement: from ἔρα, "earth," to 'Ρέα, according to Eustathios (*ad Il.* I, 55, p. 46, 20), an etymology taken up by Welcker (cf. *Griechische Götterlehre*, II, p. 216). From this point on it is easily seen how Gaia was inserted as a substitute for Rhea at the birth of the child. Another etymology connects the name with ῥεῖν, "to flow," and sees her as ὄμβρων αἰτία (cf. Scholia to Apollonios I, 1098, and *Etymologicum Magnum*, s.v. 'Ρέα). The explanation 'Ρείη = ('Ο)Ρείη, which later epithet was applied to Demeter as well as to Rhea-Cybele, is probably a later learned interpretation.

Though I might discuss a number of points concerning other deities, I shall confine myself to one, namely, Artemis, and deal with her in some detail. Artemis was in classical times "the most popular goddess of Greece" (cf. Nilsson, *Greek Popular Religion*, p. 16), at least in the cult of simple rustic people. She is the goddess of wild nature. She is associated especially with the cult of the tree, and in her worship the sacred branch plays a great part. In Arcadia we have a peculiar cult of the great goddesses Despoina and Soteira, the "Virgin" and the "Savior," really only two invocatory names for Artemis, showing what strength these ἐπικλήσεις still had to form new figures even in post-Mycenaean times. Wild animals appear in her retinue; she is Πότνια θηρῶν, the ruler of animals. The dance is customary in her cult. She is also the divinity that has to do with the fertility of men and animals. She is the goddess of childbirth under the cognomen Eileithyia and she is Kurotrophos.

Artemis Ephesia preserved the characteristics of the original goddess most clearly; one is almost tempted to say that the latter still lives on in Ephesus in classical times. It is emphasized everywhere that the Ephesian Artemis is entirely non-Greek, and that she is intimately connected with the great goddess of nature and fertility in Asia Minor, whose cult the Ionians found fully developed and quite simply transferred into their own deistic system. With the knowledge of the Minoan-Mycenaean religious system that we now possess, I do not deem it necessary for us to follow this roundabout way, since it is apparent, on the one hand, that those features which are characteristic of this Asia Minor goddess can even be found in the Minoan-Mycenaean world, and on the other hand, that certain features of the Ephesian Artemis attract special attention to the Cretan goddess.

The Ephesian Artemis is a representative of primitive nature worship. We have clear witness of this in the orgiastic elements and bloody ceremonies of her cult, which are best known to us now through the monumental work of Picard, *Éphèse et Claros*, to which I refer here. Let us only touch on certain particulars.

Her great festival, the *Ephesia* or *Artemisia*, was celebrated in the spring, in the month of Artemision, which was filled with all manner of festivities in honor of the goddess. Great *agones* took place, of which both Thukydides, III, 104, 3, and Dionysius of Halicarnassus, IV, 25, 4, speak. A sort of bullfight served as an introduction to these agones. To be sure, they are expressly confirmed at a rather late date, in Artemidoros, *Oneirokritikon*, I, 8, but there is nothing to indicate, as Picard would imply (*Éphèse et Claros*, p. 343), that they were taken over at this time from Thessaly. They were most certainly widespread in Asia Minor. They are known in Smyrna, where they lasted at least two days (cf. *C. I. G.* II, 3212); in Sinope (cf. *C. I. G.* III, 4157, 5); in Ancyra (cf. *C. I. G.* III, 4039, 45); in Aphrodisias in Caria (cf. *C. I. G.* II, 2759 b, 8), and other places. According to Artemidoros, only the most prominent youths were concerned with the *taurokathapsia*, the bringing forth of the sacrificial bulls. Heliodoros of Ephesus, *Aethiopica*, X, 28–39, has the following legend to relate about the origin of the taurokathapsia. The cult practice had been devised in a temple by a certain Theagenes, because one day when he was about to sacrifice a number of selected bulls, they took fright and broke loose. The connection with the Cretan bull games was established long ago (cf. Picard, *Éphèse et Claros*, p. 344, and literature there quoted).

Just like the ritual, the cult image of the Ephesian Artemis and the temple personnel bear witness to the primitive character of the goddess. The cult image was held in high regard, since it was believed to be very old and to have fallen from heaven—διοπετές. Originally it was a cylindrical wooden image, narrowing at the bottom, reminding one of the form of the Minoan-Mycenaean columns. Later, the upper part was given a human shape. The goddess is depicted with arms outstretched, like the divine epiphanies on our seals and rings, at times in association with a bee or a flower, and even with the double axe (cf. κυβηλίς). On both sides of her are shown animals looking up at her— lions, rams, or bulls. Her image also is decorated with figures of these animals and they constitute her emblems in later times. The lion represented wild nature; the ram and the bull, so well known to us, are the representatives of fertility and fruitfulness.

The bee deserves special attention. It is met with in classical times as a symbol even on Ephesian coins. We meet it in Crete in prehistoric times as a royal sign, thanks to the find from Mallia; it is also to be found with a human head on a piece of jewelry from Cyprus (cf. Milani, *Studi e materiali*, fig. 50), and I believe we see it on our representation no 13. Even Milani has seen something similar. He says: ". . . il trifoglio (*lotus corniculatus*) a foglie pelose secondo natura e, come credo, intenzionalmente assimilato ad un insetto volante, ad un' ape o ad un calabrone del gregge." Neustadt has collected rich material to prove the existence of "Melissa dea" (cf. *De Jove Cretico*, pp. 44 ff.). The bee is probably to be interpreted as a symbol for nurture. One finds traces of the character of the Ephesian goddess as a deity of light in classical times, especially in the moon or torch which are to be seen on Ephesian coins.

The nature of the goddess as the all-feeding deity has been strikingly expressed in her image with the many breasts. She is πολύμαστος or *multimammia*, but in this character she is not alone. We have in Anatolia many similar goddesses whose identification has not yet been established (cf. Picard, in *Eranos-Jahrbuch*, 1938, p. 77). Even if the embellishment of the breasts could sometimes be proved to belong to the dress, *ependytes*, I should nevertheless not be inclined to accept Picard's explanation that they depended from necklaces with other hanging charms or trinkets. But their shape, it should seem, is much too striking (fig. 26). Without going into detail I wish to remind you that the Amazons, ἀμάζονες, *unomammiae*, according to Plautus, *Curculio* III, 75, are intimately connected with the Ephesian πολύμαστος Artemis. Can this be merely accidental? I cannot believe so. Kallimachos, *Artemis*, 237 ff., relates that even before the temple of Artemis existed in Ephesus, the goddess was worshiped in a sacred tree—just like the tree goddess on the coin from Gortyn. To the tones of a syrinx the Amazons performed a holy dance near the tree. Later, in the classical period, women of the race of Amazons lived around the temple of the Ephesian Artemis, according to Pausanias VII, 2, 7, despite the fact that only virgins were permitted entrance to it (cf. Achilles Tatius, *Klitophon*, VII, p. 431).

If we consider the many-breasted Ephesian Artemis in relation to the Amazons, who have deprived themselves of both breasts or at least of the right one, we can come to a better understanding of this peculiar divinity. That which the devoted worshipers offer to the goddess for the strengthening of her creative powers is, in turn, visibly expressed in

Fig. 26. The Ephesian Artemis as shown in a statue in Naples and in a terra-cotta statuette in the British Museum.

the image of the goddess. The women have brought their offering, as the men theirs.[5]

In Ephesus the high priest of the goddess was a eunuch, and other temple attendants were spoken of as consecrated in the same fashion to the great deity. The high

---

[5] We have an ethnological parallel from the Amazon Islands near Yucatan, where the left breast on girls was reputedly cut away in order to facilitate their use of the bow and arrow, according to Alonso de Santa Cruz (cf. Ploss-Reus, *Das Kind in Brauch und Sitte der Völker*, 3d ed., II, p. 124).

priest Megabyzos—a common Iranian name—is to be compared to Attis in the cult of Cybele. With respect to both we are dealing with an original title of an office. Megabyzos' insignia of office were the tiara and the dress extending to the ground, reminiscent of that worn by the eunuchoid high priests on Hittite bas reliefs. We find exactly the same dress on two carved stones (fig. 27) from the Vapheio Tomb (cf. *Ephemeris Archaiologike*, 1889, pl. x, 26 and 32), and I consider it not implausible that we also have

Fig. 27. Seal stones from Vapheio, showing a man in Anatolian dress.

a high priest represented on the large signet ring from Tiryns (our representation no. 24).

In the place of first importance among the eunuchs as temple servants we are familiar with the Essenes, the kings of the bee swarm, a designation which must be understood together with the designation of the priestesses, Μέλισσαι, that is, bees.[6]

Many features in the cult of the Ephesian Artemis are common to cults of the Asiatic mother goddess. Ma in Komana, for example, was also celebrated in wild orgies, at which men castrated themselves and women prostituted their bodies. Under the title word Ἀμμάς, Hesychios implies the same circumstances. He specifies the goddess as Artemis' amma. The orgiastic character of Artemis' cult

[6] For the bee priests cf. Ramsay, *Asianic Elements in Greek Civilisation*, pp. 82 f.

is also emphasized expressly by Timotheos of Miletus (cf. Bergk, *Poetae lyrici Graeci*, III, 620), who, in a hymn composed for the dedication of the new temple after the famous Herostratian fire, designated the goddess as μαινάδα, θυάδα, φοιβάδα, λυσσάδα. The connection with Crete, however, is clearly shown from the close of the third century B.C., and undoubtedly goes back much farther. Reference to the Cretan Kouretes exists in connection with the *Artemision* in Ephesus (cf. Picard, *Eranos-Jahrbuch*, 1938, p. 83), and Lobeck believed that he had found the name of the Idaean dactyls on the base of the cult image (cf. *Aglaophamus*, pp. 1163 f.).

Nilsson gives much attention to the divine child. The Zeus child was born in Crete. He was put away by his mother and was reared by nymphs or animals. The festival of his birth was celebrated yearly, and the Kouretes, who had charge of him in his infancy, are obviously daemons of fertility, as the hymn of Praisos shows. The young Zeus was associated in Gortyn with the Tree Goddess, whose image is still preserved on classical coins. We hear of an ἱερὸς γάμος, and of the annual death of Zeus and of his grave in Knossos. In this part of the Zeus saga we have, clearly and plainly preserved, the same general vegetation cycle that is shown on our gold rings.

But how is it possible that there existed on Greek soil the same rites as those practiced in Asia Minor for the promotion of the growth of vegetation—rites of the kind which, according to the cult legend, Attis practiced on himself? Could they have disappeared without leaving any trace in the later myth development? Yet we really have shadowy traces of them. I would remind my readers of the myth of Aphrodite's birth. The Hesiodic version in the *Theogonia*, 191 f., retained in Homeric Hymn VI, represents Aphrodite as born from sea foam which arose when the genital parts of Uranos, the spouse of Gaia, fell into the sea at

Kythera after having been severed by Kronos' sicklesword. We have already noted that undoubtedly we must assume a sacrifice by substitution, since often in classical times, especially in the cults of Artemis and Dionysos, cakes baked in the form of *phalloi* were offered. Similar sacrifices are also to be met with in the *Thesmophoria* in honor of Demeter (cf. Nilsson, *Griechische Feste*, pp. 320 and 322). Significantly enough, the σχήματα ἀνδρῶν, namely, phalloi, were thrown, according to the Scholia to Lucian, into openings in the earth (cf. Rohde, *Kleine Schriften*, II, pp. 355 ff.).

The knowledge which we now have of the Minoan-Mycenaean religion gives us a new view of Demeter. It cannot be denied that even she has various characteristics that go back to the Cretan mother goddess and her parallels in Asia Minor such as Ma. Nilsson, *Minoan-Mycenaean Religion*, p. 450, denies this—unjustifiably, it seems to me—so far as it concerns Demeter Eleusinia. Picard has now answered his objection (cf., e.g., *Eranos-Jahrbuch*, 1938, p. 95). In general it seems that many cults and festivals, including the Thesmophoria, demand new treatment.

Nilsson has postulated that we have reason to suppose that the conception of the divine child and the strongly emotional character of the religious forms which accompanied it, originating in the conception of the dying and reviving vegetation, were once present in the Minoan religion. The fact that these conceptions and their accompanying rites existed in Minoan civilization has now definitely been proved by the analysis of our documents.

Mysticism, according to ancient tradition, had its chief stronghold in Crete. I shall only refer to what Diodoros has to say regarding this matter, V, 77, 3 ff. (his source is undoubtedly Epimenides of Knossos): "The inhabitants of Crete have left the following evidence that divine cults, sacrifices, and mystery rites were carried from Crete to other peoples; the dedication rites which were performed by the Athenians in Eleusis, perhaps the most famous of all, as well as the rites in Samothrace and those that are practiced in Thrace among the Kikones, whence the inventor of rites, Orpheus, comes—these were all secret, but in Knossos it was an old custom to perform these rites openly, and that which among others is done in secret is not hidden by them from anyone who desires to know about it. They say that most of the gods have gone out from Crete to various parts of the world as benefactors of mankind, giving to each and all a share in their useful discoveries. It was thus that Demeter went to Attica and from there to Sicily, and later also to Egypt. Especially in these places she enjoys an active worship from those who have benefited from her good deeds, because she has brought them corn and taught them to sow the seed."

This pronouncement of Diodoros gives us occasion for mentioning briefly the Eleusinian Mysteries. In an article which I published under the title "Der Ursprung der eleusinischen Mysterien" (*Archiv für Religionswissenschaft*, 1922, pp. 287 ff.) I have tried to point out their Cretan origin. Following is a summary of the evidence given there.

The oldest Telesteria are pre-Hellenic; the name Eleusis suggests pre-Hellenic Crete; certain cult vessels, the *kernoi*, and libation jugs are common to Eleusinian and Minoan cults; the form of the Telesteria may possibly be a further development of the so-called Minoan theater; the *anaktoron* is the same as the Cretan repositories and so-called house chapels; the purifications of the Eleusinian cult come from Crete, where they originally belonged to the Minoan religion; the kernel of the mysteries is a cult of fertility, which is also the kernel in the Minoan religion; a double ancient tradition traces the mysteries to Crete: on the one hand Diodoros, who stands independently, on the other the Homeric Hymn to Demeter, on which Isokrates as well as Dionysius of Halicarnassus and Servius are dependent. These conclusions, established nearly twenty years ago, have since been adopted by leading historians of religion. The correctness of the interpretation, achieved without the more intimate knowledge of the basic content of the Minoan religion which we now have, is further strengthened by the present research. In this connection I should like to emphasize one or two particulars to which I directed attention at that time.

Proceeding from the *Oneirokritikon* of Artemidoros, I, 8, where he says: "In Ionia young Ephesians of their own free will, and in Attica among the Eleusinian goddesses Athenian youths, περιτελλομένων ἐνιαυτῶν, and in the Thessalian city, Larissa, the most prominent of the inhabitants, fight against bulls," I draw attention to the fact that a kind of bullfight was associated with the Eleusinian cult. I find a reference to the same fact in three honorary inscriptions to ephebi, where it says, "They also led oxen at Eleusis as a sacrifice to the mysteries." As Foucart, *Les Mystères d'Éleusis*, p. 373, and Ziehen, *Leges sacrae*, p. 55, have maintained, it is a matter of the bringing of living animals, which surely could not have been done without danger. I interpret the words of Artemidoros as an implication that it was first necessary to capture the animals, even if the bringing of them to the altar was more important. I venture to see in this a survival of the Minoan bull games, exactly as we had it in Ephesus.

In the Eleusinian cult we are concerned with a pair of divinities, Θεά and Θεός—that is, they are nameless. Nilsson (cf. *Greek Popular Religion*, pp. 46 f.) interprets them as Pluto and Persephone, by whose side stand the pair Demeter and Kore. By the side of each pair there was later placed a hero, so that there were two triads, (1) the God, the Goddess, and Eubouleus, and (2) Demeter, Kore, and

Triptolemos. It is interesting to note that a seventh figure was added,—for example on an Attic relief found in Mondragone near Sinuessa, Italy,—namely, Iacchos, a personification of the cry which was heard in the great procession from Athens to Eleusis at the festival of the mysteries. This is, incidentally, an excellent example of how a deity comes into existence and takes a positive form.

The divine pair, "the god" and "the goddess," meet us everywhere in the vegetation cults; they were a survival from earlier times in the Eleusinian Mysteries and elsewhere in the Greek religion, and from there they passed over to the Roman. The union of the two may symbolize a marriage, but this notion is not always apt. I should like to direct attention especially to the twin pair, Apollo and Artemis. They have certain characters in common with the Cretan paired deities. Artemis is associated with the moon, Apollo with the sun, just as we have these two planetary bodies in association with the Cretan deities.

Another peculiar pair of divinities in classical religion is Aphrodite and Eros. I am not at all convinced that Eros is to be considered as the first personification within Greek religion. It is my opinion that he is the direct successor to the young Cretan god, closely related to Adonis and Attis, and that all of them are associated with the great Goddess of Fertility, the Goddess of Love. Here I should like to refer to the well-known fact that the Eros of Thespiai in Boeotia, according to Pausanias, IX, 27, 1, had a particularly ancient image in the form of an uncut stone. From the beginning, Eros was the most worshiped of all the gods there, and one has been disposed to find in his cult a relic of the time when the Minyans ruled in Boeotia. There are traces of a similar stone cult in Orchomenos, where the Charites were worshiped in the form of stones, and likewise in Hyettos, where an uncut stone had its place in the temple of Herakles (cf. Pausanias IX, 38, 1 and IX, 24, 3). It is significant that these stone cults are preserved in Boeotia, a region where, in my opinion, the Cretans once had a firm footing; Minos and Minyas are certainly identical denotations. The Charites were originally concerned with nature and fertility; they are deities of the same kind as nymphs and dryads. Thus we have here a trace of the same aniconic representation of deity which we meet in Minoan-Mycenaean religion. It is a well-known fact that the cult of stones persevered in Asia Minor down to classical times; a fact so well known, indeed, that I need not enlarge upon it (cf. de Visser, *Die nichtmenschengestaltigen Götter der Griechen*). To be sure, we should not forget in this connection the omphalos in Delphi, which I likewise interpret as a pre-Grecian relic.

The phallos-like stones, which according to ancient tradition were set up as gravestones in Phrygia, we can trace back to a similar function within the Mycenaean religion; note especially our representation no. 14. They afford additional support for the theory that the rites of death and fertility stand in close relation to each other, a concept behind which there lies a generalized notion of resurrection and immortality.

The Minoan-Mycenaean religion spread itself like a mantle over all the Greek area. Where the Dorians pushed in and settled, the mantle was, so to speak, torn and tattered and the old religion continued to live only in remote and partial survivals. The connection is more substantial wherever we meet with an older population, as for example in Boeotia or in Attica, whose inhabitants, as is well known, viewed themselves as autochthonous. Naturally the popular religion is in this connection of the greatest interest.

CHAPTER SIX

THE VEGETATION CYCLE AND THE NORDIC RELIGION OF THE BRONZE AGE—SUMMARY

I HAVE already made special mention of the surprising agreement which exists between some of the representations on our Minoan-Mycenaean gold rings, namely, those which picture boat scenes, and the Scandinavian rock en-

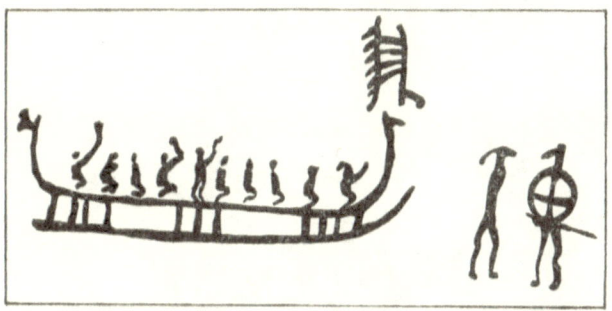

Fig. 28. Boat representation from a rock engraving in the province of Bohus, Sweden, with a man and a woman beside the ship.

gravings, especially those in the province of Bohus. Von Salis has touched on this matter in his interesting study, *Theseus und Ariadne*, pp. 38 f., without, however, attempting to demonstrate their mutual connection. I should like to sketch here, briefly, one possible explanation for the similarities that obtain.

On the rock engraving reproduced here (fig. 28) we see, among other things, a pair of figures—a man and a woman—beside a ship, in much the same position as on our ring no. 26, the woman, however, facing away from the ship as on the Tiryns ring, no. 25. Another picture (fig. 29, upper part) shows us a man and a woman embracing each other on shipboard, and over them a tree is depicted as on our ring no. 26. On a third engraving (fig. 29, lower part) the two have come together so as to be almost indistinguishable from each other, while above them hover two men with axes who are apparently performing a ritual act, perhaps in sanctification of the union.

It seems undeniable, to me at any rate, that behind representations so strikingly similar to those on our rings there

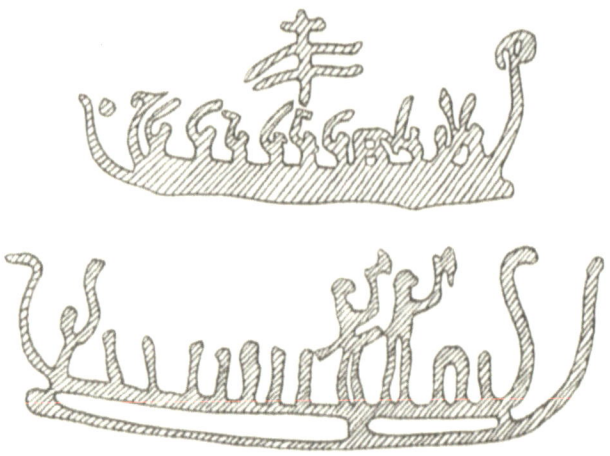

Fig. 29. Boat representations from rock engravings in the province of Bohus, Sweden, with a man and a woman embracing each other on the ship.

is some kind of connection. Many other details on the Nordic rock engravings are explicable only when we advance comparable parallels from the eastern Mediterranean region. Professor Almgren in his work, *Nordische Felszeichnungen als religiöse Urkunden* (1934), has, in my opinion, succeeded fully in establishing proof that these northern rock engravings, which come from the Bronze Age, are of religious significance. In an article, "Åkerbruksriter och hällristningar [Agricultural Rites and Rock Engravings]," *Fornvännen*, 1930, pp. 1 f., I have collected some material from Greece and the Near East which supports Almgren's theory. I only wish to mention here that the figures on the rock engravings often appear dressed in animal skins with clearly drawn tails—not swords, as they formerly were interpreted—and that quite often these skins have horns, indicating that they are bullhides. Thus is shown the close connection in which cattle, as draft animals, stood to agriculture and consequently to the magical rites of fertility in general.

The stem-handled sun disk on the rock engravings has a parallel in the mirror in the hand of the goddess on one of our gold rings (no. 6).

On some of the rock engravings there occur mutilated figures: decapitated bodies, or bodies with amputated limbs. These take us back to the Molos myth of Crete. It was Molos who, after a love affair with a nymph, was seen headless. This again is a matter of ritualistic mutilation in order to free the indwelling magical power for the strengthening of vegetative life. Such motivation agrees in its intent with the informing cause behind the Attis myth.

The pose of the suppliants on the rock engravings is also related to the analogues in Greece, in Crete, and in Egypt; that is, with the hands raised, extended. The rock engravings reveal also a similarity of symbolism in the forms used for the epiphany of the gods. Now, in view of such striking resemblance, both of motive and representation, how are we to interpret this parallelism?

Archaeological studies have revealed that as far back as the end of the Stone Age the arts of agriculture flourished, to a degree, not only in the Orient but also in Europe, and even in Scandinavia. The cereal grasses which were cultivated, namely, wheat and barley, and even millet in warmer climates, were grown originally in the Near East. The distinguished Swedish plant physiologist, Professor Sernander, has informed me that they came first from Asia Minor. From this area their cultivation spread to various regions and came in time to Scandinavia by way of the classic lands, across Switzerland, as the finds in the pole dwellings seem to indicate, and then to the North. Words such as *field, plow, to plow, sow, reap, grind*, common to South and North European languages, furnish linguistic evidence to show that along with the many samplings of seeds the most primitive of agricultural techniques were taken over as well.

We cannot hope to recapture and enter into the mental processes of those early peoples who first practiced agriculture—who first learned to strew grain in specially prepared soil and to harvest it when it was ripe. But we can endeavor to understand what a deep impression the cyclical growth of their own plantings must have made on their minds when they saw things shoot up and develop according to their prearranged design. The growth of vegetation, then, did not depend upon capricious chance, but all things developed after a certain divine order. Experience also soon taught these people that the harvests, in spite of all efforts on their part, were not of equal worth every year. It therefore became necessary to follow occult procedures whereby certain favorable factors should be brought into play to protect the crops from harmful influences. Thus, they had not only to employ their practical knowledge of the growth of crops, but must also follow out certain agricultural rituals which served as a sort of "instruction sheet," and which came to accompany the primitive agricultural methods for insuring a favorable yield. In those places where the same sorts of cereals, from a common place of origin, were raised, cultivated by comparable agricultural methods, we can expect *a priori* the celebration of an identical ritual, even though the peoples are not tribally related.

The two chief factors which determine the success or failure of crops are, of course, temperature and precipitation, that is, sun and rain. The most symbolic and profound vegetational rites the whole world over have to do with just this matter of sun worship and rain magic. The general climatic conditions of a given region will cause one or the other of these ceremonials to be the more prominent. The known similarities between the crop rites of the Old World and America and Australia depend on just this circumstance. Consequently, when we try to find an explanation of such rites, we are justified in seeking analogies from completely separate cultures. Yet these rites have a common origin only where a common concrete substratum exists, namely, the same kind of cereal plantings, which entail also the same procedure in their cultivation.

The rites we are considering are therefore just as primal as man's first great forward step toward the culture of our own times, that is, the introduction of agriculture. It is, then, self-evident that, subject as they were to multiform inner pressures and external influences, they developed in different ways; nevertheless, one is justified in finding certain traces of the same rites in the old Orient and Egypt, in Crete and in Greece, as well as in the North. Peasants and farmers in all ages are remarkable for their conservatism; it is a condition native to the rural way of life, and all religion is inherently conservative. It is no wonder, then, that certain agricultural rites have persisted for thousands of years.

Agriculture and cattle breeding are inseparable; a beast of burden is a requisite for a developed agriculture. The oldest beast of burden is the ox, first found as a domestic animal in the Orient. May we not assume, then, *a priori*, that the ox and the bull played a prominent part in the most ancient of agricultural rites, and thus find valid explanation for the special power which in their symbolic roles they inherit in the cult of fertility?

It should be added that the agricultural rites under discussion here, as represented on the Scandinavian rock engravings, do not seem to involve a formal cult instituted for the worship of a palpable deity. What we are given here is something related rather to a magical rite. By its means men wished to exert an influence upon a power, amorphous and undetermined; not to supplicate an established Divinity, free in will and purposeful.

We are confronted, however, with an interesting figure of Northern mythology, Nerthus, who deserves some recognition here. Tacitus, *Germania* 40, has left a detailed description of her cult. She was worshiped by seven peoples under the designation, according to Tacitus, of *terra mater*—which should be understood as an *interpretatio romana*. She had a sacred grove on an island in Oceanus which harbored her sacred carriage, covered and carefully guarded. Only the appointed priest dared touch it. Whenever the goddess made her presence felt, a procession, in which she was drawn by cows harnessed to this carriage, was led by her priest to the festively decorated places she desired to visit. Peace reigned during this period and all iron objects were kept confined. When the procession came full circle, the goddess was returned to her sanctuary. The carriage, before it was covered, and most likely the goddess herself before her retirement, underwent ablution and bathing in a remote lake. The slaves who attended this private ritual were, upon its conclusion, swallowed up by the waters of the lake. From this fearful and climactic scene arose the secret dread of this being, who condemned to death those who looked upon her.

The only thing we know with any assurance is that Nerthus was a goddess of vegetation—*terra mater*—whose name in normal phonetic development is comparable to the Northern Njördr. Mannhardt has pointed out the parallelism between her cult and that of the Phrygian *Magna Mater* (cf. *Wald- und Feldkulte*, pp. 571 f.). In both rituals a tour takes place in a carriage drawn by kine, in both there is the rite of lustration, in both the festival is celebrated in the spring. But Mannhardt denies what, to me, appears as of the same cult significance (cf. also Helm, *Altgermanische Religionsgeschichte*, I, p. 315). I cannot see that such a connection is wholly excluded if we accept the basic view postulated here. Both Nerthus and Njördr are deities of fertility, who are worshiped especially in the spring. The fact that Nerthus is female and Njördr male is no more curious than that Mithras is sometimes seen in female guise, sometimes in male. The gods of fertility are disposed toward bisexualism (cf. Agdistis, above, p. 107), which may later allow of fission, so to speak, in different localities. The harnessed cows are surely to be read as a symbol of a goddess of fertility. The journey of the goddess has many parallels in the most divergent places (cf. Clemen, *Altgermanische Religionsgeschichte*, p. 82). The festival of such a deity is often bound to the beginnings of navigation; and it is possible that here we get a connection of the same kind as that which is to be found in the *Dionysia* in Athens, and further, that the vehicle of the goddess was actually a boat mounted upon wheels (cf. Clemen, *ibid.*, p. 83). Let us note that the temple is situated on an island;[1] we meet this same peculiarity of locale in the Oriental cults, as we observed with respect to Zeus, Apollo, and Aphrodite; and Dea Syria, too, had her temple on an island. The priest recognized the presence of Nerthus by the signs of reawakening Nature, especially the budding of trees, and then conveyed the covered carriage. We do not know what was under the cover, whether a cult image or a sacred symbol. After the close of the festival, the goddess was conducted back to her sacred grove, and then followed the purification, apparently to be thought of as a lustration after the ἱερὸς γάμος (cf. *Archiv für Religionswissenschaft*, XIV, pp. 310 f.). The drowning of the slaves is, of course, the accompanying human sacrifice.

[1] It is hard to say which island is meant in the Nerthus myth; Rügen, Sjaelland, Alsen, Femern, and Bornholm have been suggested; cf. most recently Schröder, *Germanisch-Romanische Monatschrift*, 1934, p. 187.

To return more closely to our subject matter, even though I hold that traces of deified figures are not to be excluded from the pictured cults of the rock engravings, yet it is mainly the appearance in them of parallel magical rites that is particularly striking.

Primitive man always takes the appearance of things for their reality. By mimicry or imitation he believes that he can bring not only other men as well as animals under his control, and use their power, but also all vital or inert matter. Thus he can attain dominance over nature, whether it be the annual crop or like phenomena. But when he is dealing with abstract forces he must first expropriate their quality through the creation of visible analogies by means of image or effigy. It is this need for the concrete that accounts for the long ancestry of the image in language and art. When one fashions an effigy in wax, let us say, of the lover whose ardor has cooled, and then melts it in fire, the lover will once more be consumed by the flame of desire; when one creates an image of the sun, the quintessential substance of the sun will then be active in it; or again, when through mimicry in a ritual dance or by the imitative performance of the fundamental yet analogous process of fertility, one rehearses in its strict reality the act of copulation between man and woman, one can thus exert a comparable influence upon the impulses of fertility in nature.

Those who perform these rites are the bearers of such powers; thus they are daemons themselves, and in this character they perform all the necessary magical acts, the phallic ceremonies or the dances, to make the vegetation thrive. Let us remember that Attis was the priest's name as well as that of the god. Sometimes it is desirable to set free the magical powers contained within the bodies of the officiating actors. This results in ritual mutilation, the connection of which with fertility is quite obvious, as appears, for example, in the castration which is part of the cult of Attis.

With the fact of human sacrifice we must undoubtedly see the suggested truth, namely, that man represents a daemon of fertility whose death is followed by a resurrection whereby new and greater powers are secured for the salvation of mankind. The solar sacrifices which took place in many localities were performed also for the purpose of renewing the solar life. They took place at the very time when the sun came to renew its vital cyclical influence.

It should be added that the rites which were performed in connection with the harvest and the death of vegetation were not originally associated with the harvested crop, but were rather related to the need for the providing of new growth after the old crop was harvested. Vegetation dies and must be renewed. The daemons of fertility, embodied in the officiating priesthood, provoke new growth in nature through their phallic activity and otherwise. According to the very basic principles of homeopathic magic, the phallos and the sexual act are prerequisites for the renewal of nature. This, of course, follows upon the law of association of similarities.

If primitive man donned a mask, he was, for the time being, changed to that which the mask represented. The most customary masquerade was assumed by the wearing of an animal's skin. The magical power of the animal was seen to reside in its hide; we may point the comparison by recalling the garments of Christ, and the efficacy of innumerable other such holy relics. Clad in the hide, man exercises that magical power which is specifically associated with the animal. He who covers himself with the bull's hide becomes a bull. This animal in its role of beast of burden stands in an external relationship to agriculture, but also, through the ritual masquerading with the aid of its hide, it comes to represent agriculture by the contagion of magic. The bull's hide or its horns can represent the occult power dwelling within the bull. Here apparently is the explanation for the importance of the so-called sacral horns, the horns of consecration, in the Minoan-Mycenaean religion, where the bull, and Minos masquerading in the bull's hide, Minotaur, that is, have a leading role. The horns are thus by origin symbols for vegetative power, and only secondarily for power in general. Through the horns or their copies the strength of the bull can be transmitted to the bearer; thus we get the warrior's helmet decorated with horns.

In many religious cults there is to be found the incontrovertible connection between the rites of fertility and death rites; in the Eleusinian Mysteries, for example. The Cult of the Dead follows the general character of the Cult of Fertility, since through magical life-waking means one desires to annihilate the mortifying power which exudes from the dead person toward all about him—a power which primitive man obviously saw as an infectious disease. Here the phallos assumes its role as a gravestone. It is a noteworthy fact that the American Indians avoid burying their dead near a grain field, as I am informed by Professor Brodeur, who has himself been told this by an Indian in northern California. The same custom has also been observed in times past by the Indians in Mexico.

In the study of the forms of primitive religions, modern research deals with analogies and with an inheritance from a common home, but takes very little account of the acquisitions of peoples who are not tribally related. Yet spiritual values were transmitted among them as well as material goods. The acquisition of abstract religious conceptions and rites is certainly dependent upon such sparser traffic, when it seems to be based on a like concrete substratum. Every new and appreciable advance of culture, whether the art of agriculture or the use of metals, which has proceeded from one single source, has brought along with it as part of that new corpus of knowledge certain religious concepts and rites. These, added to the information about the actual technique of procedures, has supplied, so to speak, the directions for their use.

In Asia Minor it was held that the Great Mother had taught agriculture to mankind; the Old Egyptians maintained that Osiris had given agriculture to men and taught them to obey the laws and to worship the gods; according to the Homeric Hymn to Demeter, Demeter sent Triptolemos from Eleusis to teach men to till the soil and worship the gods. This ancient collocation of agriculture and the worship of deities is of the deepest significance for our present study.

Now, let us attempt to summarize in brief the course of our discussion. We began these lectures by establishing in outline the larger background against which we desired to see our subject, the religion of the Minoan-Mycenaean period. Naming this background the Afrasian culture world, we held that it was to be considered, above all else, as the chief seminal influence behind the great cultures which were to follow. These, in turn, could arise only with a more complex and developed agriculture. If, then, we think of these new cultures as outgrowths from a common basic culture, or specialized developments of such a culture, we can understand more readily certain of their fundamental similarities. Further, this may justify us in assuming a degree of cross-pollination intrinsic to their later flowering. It is my considered belief that in order to interpret correctly the Minoan-Mycenaean culture, no less than the Hellenistic culture of a later period, we must maintain constant care to recognize influences both from the Orient and from Egypt.

Our point of departure in the present study of the Minoan-Mycenaean religion was the classic myth of Glaukos, hitherto ignored in connection with this subject. This is the story of Minos' son who came to his death in a storage jar of honey and who, through the aid of a life-giving plant, came to life again. This myth, the basis of which undoubtedly lies in old vegetation rites, made it possible for us to read an engraving cut on a Minoan-Mycenaean gold ring which until now has defied proper interpretation. Successive analyses of a number of related representations on Minoan-Mycenaean gold rings gave us an illustrative-narrative series which proved to be demonstrably associated with a vegetation cycle. Pictured for us were the changing seasons as they were celebrated in private cult practice and official festival. We discovered analogies in the sexually mutilated worshipers within the fertility cults of Asia Minor and thereupon justified our interpretation of the enigmatic Amazons after a like fashion. At the same time we advanced proof whereby we established the significance of the Cretan bull games as integral to the ritual of the vegetation cult.

In order to gain a better idea of the divinities which are the express symbolic figures of these rites, we examined those cults of fertility and vegetation, in the religions of Asia Minor, Syria, Babylonia, and Egypt, which show a close relationship to that of the Minoan-Mycenaean. We discovered that all boast a great and universal Mother Goddess representing Nature herself, and, associated with her, a young male god representing the yearly cycle of vegetation, especially as it follows the agricultural calendar. Crete also boasts of two such comparable divinities.

This Minoan-Mycenaean religion constituted one essential element of later classical Greek religion, in which its traces remain deep and indelible. Just so does this older pre-Greek culture exist as a component of the unrivaled culture of later times. And this is as it should be. Every great culture is a mixed culture which transmutes through its own alchemy the baser metals of former ages.

Paying attention to the significance of the invocatory mode of naming deities, we saw how invocation may itself be the cause of the multiplication of myth, and the figures of myth, particularly among a people such as the Greeks, who were disposed to the concrete idea and clear anthropomorphism. The Ephesian Artemis seemed to have preserved in her cult during classical times many features of the ancient great Mother Goddess of the Minoan-Mycenaean epoch. Furthermore, some of the most impressive survivals of prehistoric times flourished on Greek soil, especially in those areas which remained unaffected by the Dorian invasions; for example, in Attica, and in Boeotia with its stone cults.

We touched very briefly on the Cretan origin of the Eleusinian Mysteries and pointed out the roles played by Θεά and Θεός. This divine pair may either be joined by marriage or be represented as brother and sister—Artemis and Apollo—or as mother and son—Aphrodite and Eros. Again, these are analogical forms of a vegetational religion, with its special emphasis on the procreative impulse.

Finally, we gave a brief outline of the diffusion of vegetation rites and their accompanying rites and deities, and tried to point out the striking similarities to be found, for example, between certain rock engravings in Scandinavia and the representations on our gold rings. In doing this we suggested that forms of ritual and worship depend on the nature of the crops and plantings which prompt them, and that they were considered as prescriptive directions for the farming and nurture of those crops in other lands.

For primitive man the task of sustaining life is the Alpha and Omega of all his actions and decisions. This applies to a savage who lives on roots and fruit as well as to a more agricultural people. The vegetation about him is the great reality; it symbolizes for him that dark, ambiguous, and irresistible impulse which causes trees to bloom and plants to grow; it is a continual reminder of that never-ceasing ordered change which brings forth whatever men and animals need for their sustenance. We can surmise the difficulty that faced mankind's early efforts at comprehending this tremendous power in all its ramifications. In order to understand and worship this power, to appease it and influence it toward beneficence, primitive man was compelled to define and shape it into concrete concepts. He came to observe that water and light are essential for vegetation; yet they remained manifestations too difficult to apprehend as objects of worship. But the sun is the giver of light, and the spring or well the giver of water. The life-giving sun is worshiped on high places where man feels himself closest to it; the spring becomes a mysterious and sacred source. The transcendental power can be influenced there, there it can be worshiped. But the spring needs a symbol or figure to represent it. An approach is made to this through associated objects, which draw attention to it from a great distance or impress it on the mind, for example the cliff from which the spring gushes forth, or the tree which grows near it. Thus, just as the wheel becomes a symbol for the sun, the tree or the stone become symbols for the well or spring: they represent the indwelling power of the flowing water or of the vegetation nurtured by it. The tree and the stone become, so to speak, the basic elements in the sacred place. One must see them as symbols or simplified images, while at the same time they stand *pars pro toto* for the sacred place and for the great supernatural power which is thus made perceptible.

These actual but not fully apprehended objects symbolize the supernatural powers. But how do they assume human form? By degrees, man grasps the fact that the same divine power which has caused the plant to grow and the fruit to ripen has also produced men and animals. Thus one no longer worships vegetation solely; the divine power is liberated, so to speak, from its sacred confines, and there is instituted the more comprehensible worship of the principle of fertility in the form of the great Mother Goddess shaped after man's own image.[2]

Thus from the bare tree trunk and the rough stone, by which once man apprehended the beneficent powers of nature and the genius of vegetation, he created, from time to time, innumerable other divinities in human form. The growth of myth, called forth by rites and cult, determines the character and incidence of divine presences. The concept of the deity depends altogether upon those inner changes and profound inclinations which stir the heart of man from age to age.

[2] For this development cf. Jean Przyluski, "Ursprünge und Entwicklung des Kultes der Muttergöttin," *Eranos-Jahrbuch*, 1938.

PLATES

1

2

3a

3

4

5

6

7

8a

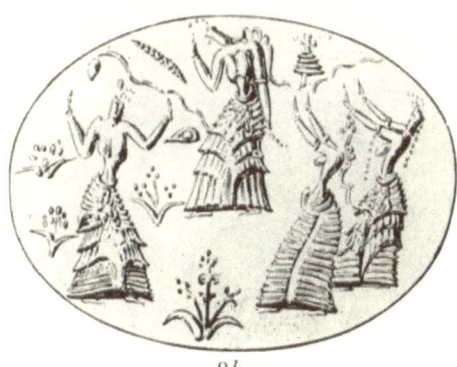

8b

9

10

11

12

13

14

15

16

17

18

19

20

21

22

23

24

25

26

27

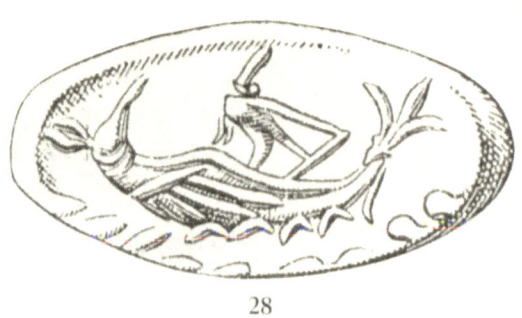

28

29

INDEX

INDEX

Adonis, 113, 115, 117, 121, 137, 140, 151; festival of, 109 passim, 116; legends, 116; myth, 119. See also Gardens of Adonis
Adoration, gesture of, 48, 51, 55, 61, 155
Aedicula, 55, 56. See also Cult buildings
Aegina, 129
Aeschylos, 11
Afrasian culture, 1, 163
Agdistis, 107, 108, 111, 159
Agenor, 132
Aglauros, 138
Agones, 97, 142
Agriculture, deity of, 99, 123, 124
Agriculture, introduction of, 2, 155, 162–163 passim
Agrimi, 53 passim
Aktaion, 118
Alexander the Great, 15, 93
Alishar-Hüyük, 13
Almgren, O., 154
Altar, 42, 103, 140
Amazons, 60 passim, 90 passim, 112, 144, 164
Amma, 106, 146
Amulet beads, 92
Anaktoron, 149
Anat, 113, 114
Ancilia, 92
Androgynous divinities, 106. See also Bisexualism
Animal, cynocephalic, 51 passim
Animal skins, donning of, 42, 98, 161
Ankh-sign, 38, 89
Anthedon, 21, 22
Anthesteria, 17
Anubis, 51, 121
Aphaia, 129, 130, 136
Aphrodite, 23, 75 n., 86, 115, 116, 119, 125, 147, 151, 159
Apollo, 7 passim, 10, 21, 69, 86, 127, 136, 151, 159; Delios, 129; Hyakinthos, 137; Pythios, 129

Apollodoros, 9, 10, 21
Ares, 19
Ariadne, 22, 81, 98, 99, 125 passim, 135
Aridela, 135, 136
Aristophanes, 11
Arkhanes, ring from, 65
Arnobius, 107, 108
Artemidoros, 142, 150
Artemis, 128, 141, 148, 151; Ephesia, 141, 142, 165; Hyakinthotrophos, 137
Artemisia, 142
Asine, 6, 14, 100 n.; rings from, 59, 65
Asklepios, 12
Astarte, 113, 116, 133
Athena, 138; olive tree of, 75
Athenaios, 137
Attica, 152
Attis, 39, 87, 107 passim, 108–109, 111, 117, 121, 137, 140, 146, 151, 155, 160; festival of, 108
Augenblicksgott, 49
Aunjetitz culture, 13

Baal, 113, 114 passim
Babylonia, 85
Babylonian culture, 43
Bee, 57, 58, 143, 144, 146
Beehive tomb, 20
Bellerophon, 23
Bird, 19, 55, 77, 88; omens, 36
Bird's-eye perspective. See Perspective
Bisexualism, 159. See also Androgynous divinities
Blinkenberg, Chr., 19
Böckh, A., 90, 112
Boeotia, 21, 152; Minoan power in, 23, 151
Boeotian plate, 75
Bow, 33, 69
"Boy God," 8, 136, 151, 164
Branch, leafy, 37, 39, 49, 51, 55, 57, 78
Britomartis, 128, 135
Brodeur, A. G., 162

[183]

Bull, 131, 132, 143, 161–162; games, 65 *passim*, 91, 93, 94, 95, 97, 98, 143, 150, 164; fights, 96, 142, 150; ring, 65; significance of the, 93, 157
Bull (constellation), 53, 93
Byblos, 85, 109, 116, 120

Campstool, 77, 79
Cassandra, 21
Cavalier perspective. *See* Perspective
Chapouthier, F., 52
Charites, 151, 152
Childe, G., 14
Chrysalis, 37, 83, 89
Circe, 118
Civilization, Minoan-Mycenaean, 5
Coiffure, 57, 67, 71
Colophon, 94
Constellations, 53, 93
Contenau, G., 134; quoted, 58
Cook, A. B., 75 n.
Corinth, 22
Crania, 73, 76
Crete, 5, 86
Cuirass, 37
Cult: procession, 56, 89, 158; carriage, 158
Cult boat, 83–85 *passim*, 153, 159
Cult building, tripartite, 40, 55, 59, 62, 100
Cumont, F., 110, 111
Curtius, L., 29
Cybele, 87, 90, 105, 106, 109, 111, 115, 139, 141, 146, 163
Cylinder seals, 51, 54, 133
Cypresses, 63, 64, 78
Cyprus, 86, 115, 143
Cythera, 86

Dactyls, Idaean, 147
Daemons, 78, 79, 147, 160, 161 *passim*
Daidalos, 128, 131
Dance (dancing), 37, 39 *passim*, 40, 42, 48, 49, 89, 110, 140, 144, 160
Dea Syria, 110, 114, 159

Death cult and fertility cult, common rites in, 42, 162
Death rites, 162
Ded, hieroglyph, 121
Delos, 7, 22, 86
Delphi, 7 *passim*, 140, 152
Demeter, 75 n., 119 *passim*, 138–139, 141, 148 *passim*, 149, 150, 163; Eleusinia, 148
Dendra-Midea, 6; gold cup from, 27; ring from, 39–40; mirror handle from, 44; goblet from, 77; glass plaques from king's tomb at, 133
Despoina, 79, 141
Deubner, L. 18
Deukalion, 107
Διάσκουραι, 72
Dikte, 129
Diktynna, 128, 129, 136
Diodoros, 108–109, 128, 140, 148–149 *passim*
Dionysia, 86, 106, 159
Dionysius of Halicarnassus, 150
Dionysos, 22, 86, 94, 108, 125, 148
Divine: child, 138, 147, 148; pair, 151, 165
Diviner's arts, 21
Dorian invasion, 152, 165
Double axe, 38, 61, 63, 72, 84, 89
Dove, 36, 115
Dress, 36, 37, 65, 67, 76, 79, 91, 110, 144, 146. *See also* Hide dress
Dryads, 36
Dümmler, F., 115

Ear, 33–34, 51, 88
Egypt, 33, 53, 61, 79, 85, 126, 134, 140, 149
Egyptian: culture, 43; royal inscriptions, 126; images, 134
Eileithyia, 130, 136, 141
Eleusinian Mysteries, 75 n., 79, 138, 148–150 *passim*, 151, 162, 165
Eleusis, 130, 149
Elysion, 130
Embalming, 15

Enclosure, 39 *passim*, 46, 52, 63
ἐνιαυτὸς δαίμων, 49
Ephesia, 142
Ephesus, 109, 141
Epikleseis, 124, 125–127 *passim*, 135, 136, 141. *See also* Invocatory names
Epiphany, 8, 19, 36, 47, 49, 64, 88, 155
Erechtheion, 138
Erichthonios, 138 *passim*
Eros, 119, 151
Essenes, 146
Eubouleus, 138, 150
Eunuch priests, 90, 109, 145
Eunuchs, 58, 146
Europa, 132–136 *passim*
Euripides, 11
Eurystheus, 19
Evans, Sir Arthur, 5, 6, 7, 9, 25, 30, 34, 37 *passim*, 38, 39, 41, 59–63 *passim*, 70, 71, 77, 79, 82, 94, 95, 100, 101, 105, 124
Eye, 33–34, 49, 88

Fertility: daemons of, 161; rites, 155, 161. *See also* Goddess of Fertility
Fertility cult and death cult, common rites in, 42, 162
Fertility God and Sun God, connection between, 85
Firmament, 39, 73
First offerings, 79
Fish, 115
Frazer, J. G., 113, 117, 121, 123
Fritze, H. von, 6 n.
Furtwängler, A., 59
Furumark, A., 26

Gaia, 141, 147
Galli, 90 *passim*, 109–110 *passim*, 112
Gallos River, 106
Gardens of Adonis, 76, 99, 115, 119
Gardner, E., 92
Gilgamesh, 117
Glaukos, 23, 136, 163; myth, 9–12 *passim*, 19 *passim*, 21–23

Gloves, 77, 79
Goblet: pedestal, 77; stemmed, 99
Goddess of Fertility, 99, 136, 151; symbol, 159
Goddess with the Mirror, 43–46
Gods, how summoned, 36, 38, 89
Gortyn, 144, 147
Gravestone, 39, 152, 162
"Great Goddess," 8, 70, 84, 99, 103, 124, 130, 136
Great Mother. *See* Cybele
Griffin, 101
Ground, indication of, 51, 56, 67, 70, 71, 72, 82
Gruppe, O., 135
Gytheion, 22

Hades, 17
Hagia Triada: sarcophagus from, 41, 42, 61, 63; cup from, 91; rhyton from, 97
Ἅλιος γέρων, 22
Harpies, 101
Harrison, Miss J., 50, 126
"Heilgöttin," 74
Helbig, W., 14, 17
Helen, 81, 99, 136
Heliodoros, 143
Helios, 131
Hepding, H., 109
Herakles, 19, 97, 151
Herkenrath, E., 71
Hermes Psychopompos, 19, 101
Herodotus, 131, 138
Herse, 138
Hesiod, 140, 147
Hide dress, 41, 42, 76, 155. *See also* Dress
Hierapolis, 116
ἱερὸς γάμος, 147
Hittites, 38, 112, 146
Hogarth, D. G., 8, 32
Homer, 14, 140
Honey, 12, 14, 15
Horace, 127
Horns of consecration, 41, 42, 43, 89, 102, 103, 162

Horus, 119, 140
Hyakinthia, 136
Hyakinthos, 136–137 *passim*
Hyettos, 151
Hyginus, 10, 19
Hymn of the Kouretes, 126
ὕμνος κλητκός, 126
Hymns, Homeric, 8, 119, 125, 147, 150

Iacchos, 151
Ida Cave, seal stone from the, 55
Idaean dactyls, 147
Ideogram, 92
Idol, bell-shaped, 49, 74, 82, 100
Indus culture, 43
Invocatory names, 113, 130–131, 135, 141, 164–165. *See also* Epikleseis
Io, 119
Ishtar, 117–119 *passim*
Isis, 85, 119, 140
Isokrates, 150
Isopata: Tomb, 20; ring from, 47

Jastrow, M., 85
Jug: beaked, 78; libation, 149
Jupiter Dolichenus, 45

Kallimachos, 128, 144
Karo, G., 81
Kernoi, 79, 149
Kilia, ring from, 67
Knife, 57
Knossos: grave of Zeus at, 39, 147; cult buildings, 41; Miniature Fresco from, 41, 49; rings from, 60, 84; Campstool Fresco from, 77, 79; seal from, 92; bull representations from, 94; Toreador Frescoes from, 94; temple of Rhea at, 140; mysteries in, not secretly performed, 149
Knot: sacral, 32, 37, 38, 61, 65, 67, 68, 79, 91, 92
Komana, 146
Kopeus, 22
Kore, 138, 150

Kouretes, 9, 92, 140, 147; hymn of the, 126
Kronos, 139, 140, 148
Kurotrophos, 141
Κυβηλίσαι, 105

Lakonia, 136
Lamp, 61, 69, 78, 131; significance of, 89
Landscape with cult scene, 64, 69, 100
Lion (daemons), 78 *passim*
Lions, 105, 143
Lobeck, Ch. A., 147
Lucian, 12, 83, 110, 116, 148
Lucina, 127
Luna, 127
Lustration, 106, 158, 159
Lycians, 23

Ma, 106, 146, 148
Magic: weather, 43; sympathetic, 62, 89, 121; sun, 62, 69, 89; rain, 106, 156; rites, 155–158 *passim*
Magna Mater, 87
"Maizweig," 49. *See also* Branch, leafy
Mallia, 100, 143
Malten, L. von, 93 *passim*, 94, 130, 132
Mannhardt, W., 158
Marinatos, S., 9, 49, 74, 81, 83, 100, 124
Mask, 161
Matriarchy, 112, 123
Matz, F., 26
Mayer, M., 57
Megabyzos, 146
Melissa dea, 144
Μέλισσαι, 146
Menelaos, 81
Metals, use of, 162
Meyer, E., 51, 112
Midas, 108
Milani, L. A., 143–144
Mingazzini, P., 129
Minoan language, 128
Minoan-Mycenaean culture, 5, and *passim*

Minos, 9, 10, 98 *passim*, 128, 131, 152, 162
Minotaur, 43, 98 *passim*, 101, 131, 162
Minyas, 152
Mirror, solar symbol, 45
Mithras mysteries, 79
Mochlos, 82, 100
Molos, 116, 155
Moon, 26, 99, 131, 136, 144; representation of, 73, 78
Moon goddess, 131, 132, 136
Morgan collection of cylinders and other ancient seals, 52, 54 n.
Môt, 114
"Mother Earth," 93, 106, 122
Mother Goddess, 33, 75 n., 123, 139, 146, 148, 164, 167
Müller, K. O., 90, 112
Müller, V., 28 n., 79
Mummification, 17
Mutilation, 155, 160; sexual, 90, 109-110, 147-148, 155, 160, 164; ritualistic, 155
Mycenae, 139; rings from, 38, 52, 53, 54, 56, 59, 62, 69, 76, 101; friezes from, 29, 78; gold plates from, 40, 56; Votivpinax from, 73
Mycenae Shaft Grave V, 16, 77
Mykerinos, 131
Mykonos, 139
Mysteries. *See* Eleusinian Mysteries
Mysticism, 148-149
Myth, origin of, in rites, 110, 115, 164-167 *passim*

Nanna, 106
Nature goddess, 87, 115, 123
Naxos, 22
Nephtys, 85, 121
Nerthus, 86, 158-159
Nilsson, Martin, 6, 9 *passim*, 33, 34, 37, 38, 43, 47, 52, 53, 61, 62, 64, 68, 70, 81, 86, 91, 93, 124, 125, 128 n., 129, 137, 138, 139, 147, 148 *passim*, 150
Njördr, 158, 159

Old Salamis, bead seal from, 63-64
Omphalos, 7, 140, 152
Orchomenos, 151
Orpheus, 149
Osiris, 85, 117, 119, 120, 121 *passim*, 137, 140, 163

Palace Style vases, 72
Palladium, 92
Pandrosos, 138
Paris, 99
Pars pro toto, 50, 166
Pasiphae, 9, 10, 131-132 *passim*, 136 *passim*
Pausanias, 107, 131, 140, 144, 151
Pelagia, 119
Pernier, L., 140
Persephone, 150
Perspective, bird's-eye or cavalier, 26, 49, 51, 53, 56, 82
Pessinus, 105-107 *passim*
Pfuhl, E., 12
Phaistos: rings from, 35, 102, 103; temple of Rhea at, 140
Phallos, 106, 107, 148, 161
Phoenicia, 116, 135
Phrygia, 39, 105, 107, 152
Phylakopi, jug from, 74
Picard, Ch., 90, 131, 142, 144, 148
Pithoigia, 17
Pithos burial, 13, 14, 32, 34, 35, 36, 38, 88, 115
Plant, life-giving, 10, 20 *passim*, 22 *passim*
Plutarch, 108, 109, 116, 120, 125
Plutos, 138, 150
Polyidos, 9, 10, 11, 20
πολύμαστος Artemis, 144
Poppy heads, 71, 74, 75, 75 n.
Porphyrius, 111
Portal shrine, 60
Potniai, 22
Pottery making and painting, 1
Πότνια θηρῶν, 105, 141
Powers, transferring of, 36

Preller, L., 15, 19, 21; quoted, 12
Prinia, idol from, 100
Prothesis, 109
Przyluski, J., 167 n.
Ptah, 33
Purification, rite of, 100, 149
Pyrrha, 107

Races, development of, 2
Ram (constellation), 53, 93
Rams, 79, 143
Rapp, A., 111
Ras Shamrah, 3, 113, 116
Reinach, S., 122
Representation, simultaneous, of successive events, 28–29, 47, 80–81
Resurrection, 109, 115, 116, 117, 121, 152
Rhea, 75 n., 115, 139 *passim*, 140
Rhyton, cylindrical, in female shape, 100
"Ring of Minos," 41, 101
"Ring of Nestor," 25, 101
Rings: representations on, 25–33 *passim*; at Oxford (no. 1), 32, 61, 64, 69, 88 *passim*; from Phaistos (no. 2), 35, 65, 82, 87, 88, 89, 91, 102, 103; from Vapheio (no. 3), 25, 36, 65, 67, 87–89 *passim*, 91 *passim*, 102, 103; from Mycenae (no. 4), 38, 87, 88, 89, 91, 92, 100; from Dendra (no. 5), 39, 55, 87, 89 *passim*, 100; in Berlin (no. 6), 43, 87, 88, 89; in Candia (no. 7), 29, 46, 87, 89, 100; from Isopata (no. 8), 47, 82, 89, 100, 103; from Phaistos (no. 9), 50, 89, 103; from Mycenae (no. 10), 52, 89, 91, 100; from Mycenae (no. 11), 53, 89; from Mycenae (no. 12), 54, 62, 71, 89, 100; from Mycenae (no. 13), 30, 55, 56, 89, 100; from Mycenae (no. 14), 55, 59, 66, 89, 100, 152; from Knossos (no. 15), 60, 67, 68, 69, 89, 90, 93, 100; from Mycenae (no. 16), 55, 62, 91, 100; in Athens (no. 17), 64, 91, 100; from Arkhanes (no. 18), 65, 66, 91, 92, 93; from Smyrna (no. 19), 67, 91, 93, 96; in Berlin (no. 20), 31, 67, 68, 69, 89, 93, 98, 100; from Mycenae (no. 21), 69, 98; from Mycenae (no. 22), 26, 55, 69, 70, 76, 82, 92, 98; from Mycenae (no. 23), 76, 99 *passim*; from Tiryns (no. 24), 25, 26, 76, 89, 99, 115, 146; from Tiryns (no. 25), 29, 68, 80, 82, 84, 85, 99, 153; from Candia (no. 26), 81, 99, 100, 153, 154; from Mochlos (no. 27), 82, 99, 100, 102; from Knossos (no. 28), 84, 99; from Athens (Minotaur Ring), 31, 101
Rites of death and of fertility, 42, 162
Rites, vegetational, 156, 161, 165. *See also* Vegetation cults
River systems, importance of, 2
Robert, Carl, 7, 104
Rock engravings, Scandinavian, 46, 153–155 *passim*, 165
Rodenwaldt, G., 29, 73
Roscher, W. H., 132 *passim*, 135 *passim*
Rose, H. J., 9

Sacrifice, human, 159, 161
Safôn, 114 *passim*
Salis, A. von, 80, 84, 153
Samothrace, 149
Sanctuaries, different kinds of, 84, 100
Sangarios, 108
Sarpedon, 23
Savignoni, L., 35, 50
Scale pattern, 102
Schliemann, Heinrich, 5, 16
Schulze, W., 130
Schweitzer, B., 31
Scilla maritima, 83
Scourging, ritualistic, 122
Seager, R. B., 82, 83, 84
Selene, 119, 131, 132, 135
Servius, 150
Seth, 120, 121
Shield, figure-eight, 37, 38, 39, 65, 73, 83, 91, 92

INDEX

Shin bindings, 35, 37, 52, 91
Ship with cabin, 80
Ship's carriage, 86
Shoes, 58
Shrine, hypaethral, 73, 75
Sidon, 133
Signet rings: impressions from, 30; arrangement of figures on, 31
Sisyphos, 22
Skin color indicating sex differences, 95
Smith, Elliot, 17
Snake, 10, 11, 20, 33, 49, 138 *passim*
Snake the symbol for water, 20, 50, 89
Solinus, 128
Sophocles, 11
Sotades bowl, 12
Soteira, 141
Space, concept of, 26
Speech, gesture of, 32
Sphinx, 101
Spikes, 71, 75, 119
Stengel, P., 14, 36
Stone, 34, 140; cult, 7, 105, 152, 166
Stratonikeia, 109
Structure with gateway, 60, 67, 82–83
Sumerian culture, 43
Sun, 26, 62, 69, 99, 131, 160, 166; representations of, 69, 73, 78, 155, 166; magic, 69, 89; worship, 156
Sun God, 69, 85, 134; connection between, and Fertility God, 85
Sun Goddess, 114
Sun symbol, 44, 166

Tacitus, 158
Tammuz, 117–119 *passim*
ταριχοι, 17
Taurokathapsia, 143
Technau, W., 133 n.
Telesteria, 149
Temenos, 33, 39, 62, 100
Thalamai, 131
Θεά, 150, 165
Θεός, 150, 165
Theagenes, 143

Theokritos, 116
Theseus, 81, 97, 98, 99
Thesmophoria, 106, 148
Thespiai, 151
Thisbe, treasure from, 101
Thot, 134
Timotheos of Milet, 147
Tiryns, 139; friezes from, 29, 92; rings from, 76, 80, 146
Tomb, 11, 20, 39, 92; beehive, 20; Vapheio, 32, 36, 146
Tree: cult, 7, 33, 141, 144, 166; shaking of, 36, 39, 89 *passim*; in burial places, 38
Tree Goddess, 147
Triptolemos, 20, 99, 138, 151, 163
Tsountas, C., 31, 53, 56–59
Tylos, 20
Typhon, 120

Underworld, Ishtar's journey to, 118–119
Universal deity, 123
Uranos, 135, 147
Usener, H., 49

Vapheio Tomb, 32, 36, 146
Vegetation cults, 105, 151
Virolleaud, Ch., 113 *passim*, 114
Volo, 40

Wace, A. J. B., 72
Water, representation of, 62, 84, 102
Weather magic, 43. *See also* Magic
Wilamowitz, U. von, 129

Xanthoudidis, 79

Yortan, 13

Zagreus, 94
Zed, hieroglyph, 121
Zendjirli, 44
Zeus, 86, 94, 107, 108, 132, 137, 139, 140, 147, 159; Labrandeus, 105, 129; Asterios, 132; Dolichenus, 134; Bouleus, 138; Ktesios, 138

www.ingramcontent.com/pod-product-compliance
Lightning Source LLC
Chambersburg PA
CBHW021708230426
43668CB00008B/765